EARLY CHILDHOOD EDUCATION

EARLY CHILDHOOD EDUCATION

DR. M. SAKKU BHAVYA

KALPAZ PUBLICATIONS
DELHI-110052

Early Childhood Education

Rs. 720

ISBN: 81-7835-569-8

Published in 2007 in India by
Kalpaz Publications
C-30, Satyawati Nagar,
Delhi-110052
E-mail: kalpaz@hotmail.com
Phone : 9212729499

Lasser Type Setting by: Rudra Computer Graphics, Delhi
Printed at : Salasar Imaging System, Delhi

Dedicated to My Parents

List of Tables

(Frequency Distribution and Percentages Chi-square Values)

Contents

List of Tables

(Frequency Distribution and Percentages Chi-square Values)

Acknowledgements

Research, unlike any other academic activities, needs constant encouragement, support and inspiration to sustain. In this research activity I have incurred many debts, tangible and intangible. Some of them are mentioned here.

I place my deep debt of respect and gratitude to **Dr. Mary Kutty Thomas**, my research supervisor, for her benevolent and able guidance in carrying out this academic exercise to its timely completion. I remain indebted to her for her sympathetic and appropriate attitude towards the successful completion of present piece of work.

I extend my deep sense of gratitude to **Prof. V.B.B. Sarma**, Dean Faculty, of Education I.A.S.E, Osmania University, Hyderabad for his motivation and continuous encouragement and timely help.

I expresses my gratitude to **Prof. S. Paramaji** for his valuable guidance in this work.

I profusely thank **Prof. S. Sreedhara Swami** and **Prof. Sudhakar** for their valuable suggestions.

SAKKU BHAVYA

1

The Problem: Theoretical Frame of Reference

1.0. Introduction

The arguments in favour of Early Childhood Education are as varied as they are numerous. They range from economic argument of greater productivity and the ethical argument of the right to live and develop potential to the fullest through to the social argument of greater equality between classes and sexes; to the scientific argument of greater intelligence and more balanced social behaviour and to the political argument of greater participation in society. Each argument has its own debate but all require a sustained wholistic Early Childhood Education intervention.

Realizing the crucial importance of the rapid physical and mental growth during the early childhood the Government of India has sponsored a number of Early Childhood Education (ECE) programmes particularly after National Policy for Children 1974. The existing ECE programmes include :

1. Integrated Child Development Service (ICDS)
2. Scheme of Assistance to voluntary organizations for conducting Early Childhood Education (ECE Centers)
3. Balwadies and Daycare Centers run by voluntary agencies with Government Assistance. Day care centers will be provided as in support services for universalization of primary education to enable girl engaged in taking care of siblings to

attend the school and as support for working women belonging to poor sections.

4. Pre-primary Schools run by State Government and Municipalities Government and Non Governmental Agencies.

Urban Community Development is a new venture in India. The planning commission has decided to introduce Pilot Projects based on the recommendations of the Rural Urban Relationship Committee set up by the Ministry of Health. The objectives of Urban Community Development as defined in the scheme are as follows:

(a) Creating a sense of social coherence on a neighborhood basis through corporate civic action and promoting a sense of National Integration.

(b) Developing a sense of belonging to the Urban Community through increased participation of the people in community affairs and promoting a way of thinking that they should concentrate first on solving problems with their own initiative, organization, self help and mutual aid.

(c) Bringing about a change in attitude by creating civic consciousness and by motivating people to improve their conditions of life.

(d) Developing local initiative, identifying and training of local leaders.

(e) Ensure fuller utilization of technical and welfare services by helping the community to locate what help can be had from the Municipality or other organizations and how to get it, and what assistance and guidance can be obtained from government and higher levels and how to approach them.

Hyderabad city is situated at 17.278, latitude and 78-27E, longitude and is with an average altitude of 1778 feet above the mean sea level. It is about 92 miles from Bombay, 491 miles from Madras and 987 miles from Calcutta by Rail.

The Twin Cities of Hyderabad and Secunderabad stand on Pink and Grey Granite which is suitable for building constructions.

The area of Hyderabad city (Municipal Corporation) spreads over an area about 192 sq. kms. and forms a part of Hyderabad District. Hyderabad City is the capital of Andhra Pradesh and is the 6th largest city in the country.

The Urban Community Development (UCD) project in the MCH was sanctioned as a Centrally Sponsored Scheme in the year 1967 covering only 50,000 population has multiplied into 12 projects covering entire city population. Every activity of UCD is directed towards bringing about a social change. The programmes are decided on the basis of the felt needs. The self help activities mentioned under the objectives of UCD are linked systematically with Governmental programmes would bring faster social change and can go beyond simple local projects to major programmes of educational significance. The UNICEF association with this project brought about major social changes in the families. The project worked under the General Administrative control of Commissioner/ Special Officer MCH but under direct control of the director (Rajagopala Chary: 1983).

The demand for the expansion of the project in the late sixties and early seventies could not be resisted as it caught the imagination of both the municipal corporation and the people who found in it an answer to their felt-needs. The urge to expand the coverage of the project on the part of the Municipal Corporation synchronized with the demands of the people who felt that the Project Staff reached their levels to serve cater to their expressed felt-needs.

The State Government being satisfied with the useful service rendered to weaker sections by the UCD and based on the request of the MCH, Hyderabad for expansion of the programme, sanctioned two additional projects in the year 1974. Apart from the above projects, three satellite projects were started around the main projects to cater to the demands of the adjacent areas to have benefit of the programme.

The UNICEF who were associated with the UCD project Hyderabad right from 1969 by way of studies and survey of the UCD programmes and its impact on the people particularly women and children, offered assistance for expansion of the programme in all wards of the M.C.H. Hyderabad. A scheme for covering the M.C.H. area and twin cities under 12 projects was drawn and submitted to the UNICEF through the State Government and Government of India (Rajagopala Chary: 1983).

Now the UCD programme is functioning with 12 projects as an integrated programme for the physical social and economic development of the people particularly living in the slums and backward pockets in present plan of action, 1980-81 to 1984-85 and the Urban Community Development project has been receiving assistance from the UNICEF at the rate agreed to in the plan of action.

The present cost per annum on the project is about Rs.30,00,000.00 against which the state grant is Rs.7,00,000.00, UNICEF grant is Rs.7,80,000.00 and the balance is met from the funds of the Municipal Corporation of Hyderabad (Rajagopala Chary: 1983).

Self help has been the philosophy of the Urban Community Development project since the beginning. The project proceeded on the assumption that any neighborhood no matter how poor can do something to improve itself by its own efforts and that any approach for outside help should be resorted to only after it has exhausted its own resources fully.

The success of the project depended almost entirely upon the work of each individual community organizer who had to stimulate guide and sustain the whole process by working with individuals and groups and bringing in outside help when needed. The task required a great deal of patience sensitivity and commitment to the aims of the project.

1.1 Educational Programmes

Child as the nucleus for social coherence, motivation, social change, community belongingness and people's involvement.

Balawadee programme intended to mould the child at the preschool age. Educational programmes like Balawadees , Creches, Anganwadies, Coaching Centers, Adult Literacy Centers, Reading Rooms and Libraries, Community T.V. Sets under matching grants, film shows etc. in slums are taken up based on the local needs and peoples involvement. The Balwadies and Anganwadies cover the children of the age group of 3 to 6 years while the creches are for the children below 3 years. Health care, Nutrition, Physical Development, Literacy, Development of Sports and Cultural Talents inculcation of good habits and decipline are taken care of at these centers which are run in collaboration with the Local Voluntary Organizations. The Anganwadies have been working under the ICDS and Urban Community Development Project co-ordinates with local voluntary organizations.

Activities like the Adult Literary Centers, Self Help Reading Rooms and Libraries and Community T.V. sets supplied in slum areas have been found useful in bringing the local communities particularly the youth together resulting in exchange of views and organizing activities of mutual interest and community benefits and also to reduce social tensions. These successes are indications of the community efficiency in running them.

1.2. Significance of the Study

There is a growing awareness not only in India but through out the world of the crucial significance of the years of early childhood education for the optimum development of child. A number of research studies and the intervention programmes that focus on the pre-school child indicate that the foundation for later development laid in the early years and that impoverishment suffered at this stage is likely to damage severely subsequent development of the child. Particularly in India the problems encountered at this stage are stupendous. First of all, we have approximately one fifteenth of the total population in the age group of 0-6 years. The rate of infant mortality is very high. Malnutrition is another major problem, which complicates matter and leads to increased mortality and morbidity in young children. After elementary stage the problem that has been ploughing our schools for the past thirty years is the higher rate of wastage and stagnation which is at its worst in the early primary classes where it is as high as sixty percent. Only forty percentages of children entering Class I reach Class III without any break. This leads to colossal wastage of resources and what is more utter negation of all efforts for universalization of elementary education. Another problem peculiar to many developing countries including India is the low rate of adult literacy and severe poverty of the parents. Most of the children, thus, by and large are deprived of stimulation at home as the parents being poor and illiterate and not in a position to give them much support. Thus, it reduces itself to the fact that the responsibility to give stimulation and compensatory education has to be borne by the organized institutions such as Early Childhood Education Centers. Early childhood education is now assuming dual importance. First it has direct influence on child development, second its potential contribution to the programme of Universal Elementary Education. This contribution has two functional aspects one is that the child receives care and second is that his/her young caretaker usually a girl child is freed to attend the school. The latter outcome removes one basic cause of drop out.

It has now been adequately shown through research that the way children respond to their environment and develop their learning capabilities are consequences of the nature of nurture, nourishment and stimulation received from the foetal stage through their early years. The maximum process of the brain development of the child occurs during the first three years of life. The need for children to receive appropriate stimulation, emotional security and fulfillment of their basic physical needs of nutrition, health and protection from the very beginning cannot be underestimated.

Family structures all over the world continue to change in response to industrialization, urbanization, population growth, increasing longevity and migration. While these changes have created new opportunities, they have also disrupted familiar cultural practices and survival patterns that families have developed over the years to cope with their multiple responsibilities.

In the past few years, joint family norms are being forsaken and the nuclear family system has made several comprehensive demands on the skills of family members, depriving children the opportunity to understand extended family and older generation who can give care and emotional support. One aspect of life affected by these trends is the inability of the family to provide optimal child rearing environments in the context of widespread changes in the social fabric of families, neighborhoods and communities.

Rapid economic changes have not only led to marginalization with consequent changes in the social structures of urban and rural communities, but also changing life styles that cut across all sections of society. In their struggle for survival the knowledge of communities with respect to child rearing is not only being eroded but also more alarmingly, being replaced by undersirable practices.

Safety nets of health and nutrition have been set up by Government, attempting to ensure basic minimum standards of survival and growth of children of the deprived communities. However, much more still needs to be done in these areas as well as in areas of the psychosocial inputs, so essential for the integrated and wholistic development of children as human beings. The educated woman either for economic reasons or aspiration is, for most part of the day, unavailable for her child and is dependent on institutional care/family support thus deflecting/diluting her role as mother and primary care giver. The commercial myopic focus of schools has necessitated a redefinition of early child rearing.

To Increase Knowledge Base

- Gather, synthesize and disseminate information on child development

- Draw from field experience, traditional wisdom and scientific research
- Identify communication channels
- Keep up to date with the latest research worldwide on ECCD
- Interactive stimulation process so vital to holistic child development.
- That the life cycle approach of interventions at each stage of the child.
- Development is essential for accelerating and building on earlier positive actions.

To Build Bridges

- Faster networking with those with common concerns and interests
- Work across sectoral divisions
- Put people in touch with the work of others, with organising meetings, working forums, publications etc.
- Serving as a communication point.

To Serve as a Sounding Board

- Dialogue with funders and decision makers about issues of parenting
- For policy formulation, programming planning and implementation.

To Support Efforts

- Strengthening capacities of child rearing in parents and communities
- For creating a positive nurturing environment for all children and especially from deprived and unreached communities.

To Propagate on

- Culture specific and holistic child rearing practices
- Developmentally appropriate stimuli
- Impact of positive and negative parenting
- Rights of the child
- Coping capabilities of caregivers

- Community based child care services as complimentary rather than alternate to parenting.

To Focus on

- Stages of parenting - parental readiness, planning for parenthood, pregnancy, preparing for safe delivery, early years of the child.
- Trauma of rejection based on gender, disability, colour, ordinal position etc.
- Equalising gender opportunity.

Parenting is Trusteeship not Ownership

All parents want the best for their children. They are in a position to be the best observer of and, consequently, are best able to provide for the physical and psychological needs of their children. Children need to be exposed to certain environmental experiences/interactions for optimal development to take place and Parents and caregivers will provide these experiences if they know how to and why they are important. Since there is no one way to rear children, each culture has developed its own method of parenting.

To enhance the quality of parenting parents must have some knowledge of basic child rearing tools.

1. Knowledge about Child Development:

- Children's normative patterns
- Stages in physical, social and language development
- Nutritional and health needs at various stages
- Emotional needs and typical early social-emotional behaviour.

to forestall inappropriate parental responses to their emotions and behaviour.

In view of the need and significance of ECCE the researcher has choosen to study the working of Balawadees in Twin cities of

Hyderabad and Secunderabad. Where a number of such institutions are established and run in cooperation with several agencies

1.3. Children are Natures Gifts to Human Kind

Teacher education essentially being an enterprise of initiating one to a profession involves provision of theoretical learning and insights from the contributory disciplines, development of proficiency competency and skills to carry out effectively the professional functions and building of proper professional values, attitudes, interest and appreciations. Every effort must be made to optimally integrate theoretical learning with practical experience.

Teacher preparation has been visualized as a professional programme aiming at development of the teacher as a person and as an agent of social change. This concept of teacher is sought to be achieved through implementation of the suggestions and recommendations confined in this teacher education curriculum frame work.

The pre-service teacher education programme for all levels has been visualized keeping in view the importance and requirement of elementary education which comprises two distinct levels primary and upper primary a two year duration of teacher training has been visualized after plus two stage of education. Integrated programmes of teacher education have not yet taken roots in the country except in the regional colleges of education of the NCERT. The concept of working with the community as an important component of teacher education curriculum at all stages has been integrated with the practical aspects of the foundational courses in education.

Forty one percent of the population of India are children as per the census of 1971. If you try to study a nation, first you have to understand the condition and status of the children in that country. They are the main factor to determine the future of the country. Their health, their education, their individuality, their mannerism, their behavioural atitudes towards the society etc, are to be attributed to the future development of a nation. Children are the most precious nature's gift to humankind.

The child is a developing person and is in continuous need of care, stimulation and nurturing. These should be provided by parents, the family and the society at large. But with the collapse of traditional social security arrangements more and more children are deprived of parental and family care. As a result, millions of children are thrown away to the streets or to the cold cradles of some charitable institutions. Now there are more than 30.80 million children in our country who have been disowned by their parents because of destitution or poverty, death or desertion of one or both parents. Of the 30.80 million children, in need of care and protection, only 3 percent are in about 1500 statutory and 3000 non-statutory children's institutions in the country. In addition, roughly 20,000 children and young persons below 18 years are in jail along with adult prisoners in the country. Of all these children and young persons, 80 per cent are boys. Of all the children and young persons in need of care and protection, 40 per cent are destitute and 25 per cent are orphaned without any adult protection or care. And contrary to common preconceptions, of all the children in need of care and protection, only 30,000 are delinquents, among the delinquents, only 8 per cent are girls. As their parents are unable to adequately fulfill their parental responsibilities, these children become the responsibility of the society and the state.

In every town and city, in our country amidst opulence and plenty there are a large number of street and working children. They are robbed of their childhood pleasures and adult protection and are prone to crime, misery, abuse and exploitation. Deprived of life, affection and sympathy of a family and subjected to exploitation, abuse and unhealthy living conditions, these children develop a strong sense of inferiority and insecurity, which create in them, fear, anxiety and guilt which in turn affect their mental health and well-being.

The children on the streets, obviously are also deprived of the educational and intellectual development. Even if they have received some education, they lapse in to idiosyncracy, since circumstances have made them dropouts of the schools over a long period of time. This is the state when the most important direction in the chapter on the directive principle of the State policy, in the Indian constitution being that the State will endeavour to give free and compulsory education to every child in the age group of 6 to 14 years of age.

Most often street children fall victims to social evils like drug addiction and are used by the drug mafias for smuggling drugs. They fall victims of organised Mafia who force the children into begging and the children some times are made handicapped for forced begging.

The Supreme Court of India has declared that definition of right to life, which is given in the Article 21 is the backbone of Indian constitution, that the right to life means the right to live with dignity and the right to privacy. But the street children of India have neither dignity nor privacy in their lives. They are subjected to life of extreme humiliation, miseries and darkness.

Article 3 of the Universal Declaration of Human Rights provides:

Everyone has the right to life, liberty and security. Article 5 of the Declaration provides:

No one shall be subjected to torture or to cruel, inhuman or degrading treatment or punishment.

Article 6 (1) of the International Covenant on Civil and Political Rights provides.

Every human being has the inherent right to life.

This right shall be protected by law. No one should be arbitrarily deprived of his life.

But with all these statutes and legal protection, in practice, the street children are deprived of their dignified and secure life.

All children in the streets work to survive. A survey conducted in Bombay shows that 71% of street children were found to be simply looking for income to support themselves and their families. Some came to the city to support their families. Some came to the city to support their impoverished families in the country side. Most street and working children were found to be law abiding, but there was no protection against extortion, physical abuse and subjection to indignity and brutality by police and other authorities, which for them was part of their way of life. As we have seen all children of the streets work to survive, there are a large number of children living with their families are sent to labour in farms and factories or the streets instead of schools. This is not a phenomenon existing only in a poverty ridden country like India. The World Development Report 92-93 of ILO states that millions of child labourers are there, even in developed countries like USA, UK, Italy, Spain and Belgium. After the collapse of Soviet Union and after the resurgence of capitalisation in that country child labour is increasing in alarming dimension there also.

Millions of children are there in India who are deprived of all their rights and compelled to work for their and their families livelihood. The largest number of child workers are in India. The reason can be attributed to the prevailing poverty and illiteracy. Inadequate agricultural reform laws and ever increasing unemployment may be some other reasons. Learning and play are the essential ingredients for the balanced development of a growing human being. When work is imposed upon the child against his or her wishes, at the cost of learning and play it becomes exploitative in nature. The miseries of working children of Delhi have been listed below as per the findings of a study conducted by national labour Institute, Child Labour Cell: 1992.

(1) Starting full time work at too early an age, (2) Too many hours spent at work which prevent the child from attending school because of lack of time and excessive fatigue, (3) Work that results in excessive physical, social and psychological strain upon the child, (4) Work and life on the streets or in factories in unhealthy

and dangerous conditions, (5) Inadequate remuneration for work and (6) Inhibition of Child's self confidence and self esteem.

According to the 1981 Census 13.6 million children are in the labour force. 11.2 million are main workers and 2.4 million are marginal workers. In 1983, National Planning Commission had projected the number of child workers at 17.36 million. The finding of a sample survey conducted by the Operation Research Group in 80-81 was that the working children in India are 44 million. But the unofficial figure amounts to more than a 100 million.

A clear understanding of the problem at various levels in the society is the first step in the elimination of child labour second is to provide facility for Pre-primary Education. In the process of the formulation of any programme or action plan, one should have a thorough understanding of the existing reality.

The most important issue is whether the society is really aware of the seriousness of the problem and whether it has a will to solve the problem.

1.4 Literacy Rates and Awareness among Women

In Indian culture, the woman is considered as Sakthi, the Goddess. In ancient India, women had a respectable position in the social setup. Gradually due to the male domination of the society the woman was degraded and her position in the society was that of a slave. Even after all the so called women's liberation movements her position, more or less remains the same. Even though one half of the population in our country is women they form the largest vulnerable group in the country, suffering life long discrimination at home, the work place and in the community and their marginalisation is further aggravated if they belong to lower caste and class, rural or minority groups.

It is not denying that the women in India today have achieved or is struggling to achieve new freedoms and new place in society. Many doors are opening to her work in many fields, her vote can sway elections education is expanding her universe. She is exhilarate by the new freedom but not yet secure in it.

Many married women are trapped in dehumanising personal situations in the family. They persist in tolerating battering, humiliation and physical and mental cruelty. She is compelled to continue to suffer this torment, as most often she will not be accepted by her parents. She remain vulnerable to continued violence or degraded status at home or exploitation and social prejudice. Battering of younger married women in families by spouses or in-laws may be linked to the horrific circumstances of dowry extortion. A tragic toll of 5817 dowry deaths were officially reported in 1993. Most often the culprits could not be booked due to the illicit nexus between the police and the husbands or in-laws. Most women suffer in silence because they know that they are powerless, as most of the indignities and deprivations are perpetuated by the very institutions and authorities meant to protect the rights. Other marginalised group are the victims of rape and sexual harassment. The number of rape case reported in 1993 was as high as 11,242 along with 2098 cases of molestation and 12, 009 cases of eve-teasing Victims of rape, instead of getting sympathy, support and justice are usually being socially ostracised and confront unspeakable prejudice from the police and judiciary.

Another most vulnerable group are the commercial sex workers. The girls and women who are economically and socially the most marginalised are often forced to adopt the profession to escape destitution caused by desertion, abuse, neglect or poverty. A UNICEF report estimates that 30% of all prostitutes in Six major cities in India were below the age of 20 and also 40% of these prostitutes entered the profession before 18 years of age.

Child prostitution is also not uncommon in India. As per the report published in 'Times of India', there are about 4 lakh child prostitutes in India, who are most destitute and even the abducted children who are sold to flesh traders. These prostitutes get infected with STD and even HIV, as they most often have no access to health care facilities (Gita Ramaswamy, 1996).

Therefore, any plan to improve literacy rate should include increase in awareness among women.

1.5 The Need for a Quality Early Intervention Programme

A programme developed with a wholistic approach using the value based contributions of research in science and technology from the West and that of the traditional child rearing legacy of the East enriches the quality of services and thereby provides a meaningful life to the child in need.

A programme based on the needs of the individual and the values of the society in which it is being implemented answers the questions : what is the content of the programme? who is the recipient? what is the methodology ? where is it to be implemented? at home, at school or centre of both locations ? who is the person providing it ? and above all how is the assessment and evaluation to be done, quantitatively and qualitatively ?

Early children development is a time of opportunity and learning. It is a process when the child unfolds behavioural patterns from immature to mature, which enables the child to emerge from a dependent entity to an independent adult. The more a child receives, better his intelligence, his personality and his growth and development.Therefore the need for more protection, care, affection, interaction, stimulation and learning. These are the rights of the child and not mere concessions.

The efforts, therefore, should lie in advocating a rights-based strategy which should respond to a vision of children in the 21st century who are respected, protected and loved. In order to ensure the best interest of the child it is essential to guarantee his economic, social, cultural and civil rights. More importantly every single child ought to be guaranteed equality of opportunities without any distinction and this could perhaps come from the creation of a caring community, right from the parents to guardians, to care providers, to neighbours, to peer groups, to policy-makers and implementers.

We are all aware of the fact that India has been a signatory to CRC. The ratification of the CRC implies obligation on the State Governments to respect, protect, facilitate and fulfil rights as embodied in CRC. It also implies that the unreached should be reached, specially those belonging to SCs, STs, those disadvantaged due to socio-economic and socio-cultural factors, the neglected and all the juvenile delinquents, etc. It also implies moral obligation on the family and community to provide care and protection because many of the violations of child rights take place within the household, and sometimes with the knowledge of the community. This is particularly with regard to issues of protection such as child suicides, child abuse and their sexual exploitation. Kerala, as the entire nation is aware of, has gone for a massive decentralisation of democratic authority, where 40% of the State's Plan funds have been given to the local bodies for implementation at the local level. The objective is that through local initiative, the effort should aim at effective delivery of services, increased accountability and openness and transparency in decision making. Towards achieving this end, monitoring by People's Committees as in the case of Panchayath committees should be strengthened which act as watch dogs in Kerala.

1.6. Child Development and Nutrition Programming

While talking of ECD, one might not forget that malnutrition among young children remains as one of the most difficult and complex goals. The effort, therefore, should be on reducing malnourishment by reaching out to children in the most crucial age group of under three years and focusing on caring practices in the household, improving access to health care and a safe environment, reducing gender discrimination and enhancing the nutritional status of the adolescent girls.

- Recognise that the child's right to survival, development, protection and participation is universal and with no discrimination whatsoever,

- Ensure that every child is healthy, well nourished and cared for and able to achieve full development potential and active learning capacity, so as to give the best possible start to life for the young child.
- Develop mainstream community-based approaches to ECD for children under three years of age.
- Enhance the capabilities of care-givers.
- Increase family and community participation.
- Strengthen 'Joyful learning' in anganwadis and Balawadees.
- Strengthen linkages between the anganwadi and Balawadees, the primary school and the health care system.

In Kerala, low birth weight among infants is an important indicator of the risk of malnutrition. It is also emerging as a major cause of chronic illness later in life, as well as a factor in mental retardation. Therefore, better care of adolescent girls and women, especially during pregnancy, would be vital in improving the nutritional status of both women and children. These pre-birth factors have to be addressed to within children development and nutrition programming of the State.

A child rights framework would, therefore, include a strong networking between Governments and the civil society, specially the women, the youth and local Govts., enabling and empowering them to identify their own opportunities and design specific interventions that are best suited to local realities.

Psycho-Social stimulation and child parent interaction has a very significant implication for physical and cognitive development of the child. Neglect of children, specially at the age less than 3 years, has serious implications in terms of over all development, readiness for schooling and learning capacity in the child. Therefore, the right of all women to be informed and counselled on appropriate infant and young child feeding practices needs to be recognised and implemented. There is need to enhance the health awareness and information among women, higher level of maternal utilisation of the health system and greater decision making roles of women in the households compared to their counter parts in the rest of the country. What would be important, therefore, is to channel their interest towards encouraging a parent-child interaction and psycho-social stimulation for the child, especially the under-twos.

In order to achieve these objectives, the tasks would include developing and testing community based approaches for children under three years, strengthening the decentralised planning that is already in progress, encouraging action research, facilitating networking civil society partners, to articulate, establish and demonstrate quality standards for ECD, promoting scaling up of early joyful learning activities with the help of DPEP, developing communications strategy and concentrating on training of functionaries and assuring the right of every child to safe water and a clean environment. One must also realise that a strategy to fulfil child development and nutrition rights needs to be inter-sectoral and therefore there is a need to focus efforts to address 'pre-birth' causes of malnutrition by focussing on adolescent girls as stated earlier.

1.7 Empowerment of People at the Grossroot Level

Not to sound pompous, it is important to repeat that Kerala has the lowest birth and death rates in India and has more hospital beds relative to the population than any other state. The rate of immunisation is highest in India, and the current rate indicate that girls are immunised at the same rate as boys. The rate of literacy among persons in the state who are 7 years old and above is more than 90%. One of the most radical implementation of land reforms in India has taken place in Kerala. There have been important achievements with respect to the abolition of untouchability. Women in Kerala have made outstanding gains in the sphere of health and education. Kerala has the best public food-distribution system among Indian States. The circulation of newspapers is more widespread in Kerala than elsewhere in India.

The tasks of realising the goals and objectives associated with multi-dimensional and inter-linked needs of children are time bound and cannot remain unattended. The prevailing situation certainly exemplifies the challenges before us to promote early childhood development, as in the development of children lies the strength of a nation. The vision therefore, would be an environment where no child would be deprived of childhood and where the child would grow in a healthy, discrimination and crime free and a safe and hygienic environment in the next millennium.

The last decade had seen many changes in our approach to programming for children having significant and far reaching implications for the future. Most important has been the shift of approach in programme from welfare to a developmental perspective, moving progressively from looking at our children as population groups whose needs have to be met, to seeing them as human beings with rights. This means that we recognize that every child has a right to survival, development, protection and participation without discrimination - regardless of their location, gender, socio-economic grouping, prevalence of other disadvantageous conditions, for example disabilities, etc. This also means that we have an obligation to transform those rights into reality.

The second major shift in the programme priorities for young children, was the realisation that if child rights must be fulfilled, a sector based approach would have to give way to an integrated and wholistic programme.

- Parents have the first responsibility with Government providing support to parents for carrying out these responsibilities.
- State to substitute for parents in specific situations.
- Ensure fundamental rights such as health, nutrition, education, protection, etc.

To achieve National and State objectives, the greatest challenge, was to reach all children and women especially from the most difficult to reach groups, and focus on the younger child (prenatal to under two years of age) and the girl child. Success lay in developing and strengthening partnerships.

There is need for a radical and generational change. It was no longer morally acceptable to 'condemn' children to a life of malnutrition, ill health or illiteracy. The need was more than ever to invest in ECCD. Many partners as possible, to join strengths in the sub-region and to give shape to that 'vision' for the young child through the agenda of early child development.

Developmental Domains

Motor	:	*The ability to move and to coordinate muscles*
Cognitive	:	*The ability to think, reason, and solve problems*
Linguistic	:	*The ability to communicate*
Social	:	*The ability to relate to other people*
Emotional	:	*The ability to feel and recognize emotions*

1.8 Objectives of the Present Study

1. To find out and assess the opinion of community members and parents on the infrastructure facilities available under the Urban Community Development Educational Programme (UCDEP) in Balawadees.

2. To find out the opinion of community members and parents on the health care facilities existing in Balawadees under UCDEP.

3. To enquire into the opinion of community members and parents on the suitability of the curriculum of Balawadee centers under UCDEP.

4. To study the opinion of community members and parents on the monitoring pattern followed in Balawadee centers under UCDEP.

5. To study the opinion of community members and parents on the Quality of Infrastructural facilities available in Balawadees under UCDEP.

6. To understand the opinion of community members and parents on the Teacher participation existing under Balawadee System of UCDEP.

7. To find out the opinion of community members and parents on the Learning Environment existing in Balwadees under UCDEP.

Hypotheses :

Corresponding to the objectives stated, the following hypotheses are formulated :

(i) There is no association between the opinions of community members and parents on the infrastructural facilities existing and the attributes of respondents like age, gender, caste, religion, education, income and occupation.

(ii) There is no association between the opinions of community members and parents on Healthcare facilities in the Balawadees and the age, gender caste, religion, education, income and occupational facts about respondents.

(iii) There is no association between the opinions of community members and parents on Curriculum Contents followed and the different attributes of respondents like age, gender, caste, religion, education, income and occupational qualities.

(iv) There is no association between the opinions of community members and parents on monitoring pattern followed and, the attributes of respondents like age, gender, caste, religion, education, income and occupational qualities.

(v) There is no association between the opinions of community members and parents on the quality of infrastructural facilities existing in different Balawadees and the age, gender, caste, religion, education, income and occupational qualities of the respondents.

(vi) There is no association between the opinions of community members and parents on teacher participation in the Balawadees schools and the attributes of respondents like age, gender caste, religion, education income and occupational qualities.

(vii) There is no association between the opinions of community members and parents on learning environment existing in Balawadee Pre-primary schools and the age, gender, caste, religion, education, income and occupational background of the respondents.

2

The Review of Related Literature

2.0 Introduction

The problem of Early Childhood Care and Education (ECCE) received comparatively greater attention due to changing global trends and challenges. Current trends of Education for All (EFA) and the role 'of ECE as a support programme for EFA have led to generating more interest in programmes for pre-school children. This is primarily because of the accumulating scientific evidence that powerfully demonstrated the importance of the early years of the child's life for subsequent development and the high development cost of inadequate care. Added to this, is the current trend of constant migration of people from rural to urban areas, the break up of the joint family system and mother's employment outside the homes which have necessarily altered the age-old child care practices and created a need for institutional care and education for the young child.

The three major international events in recent years that helped to focus attention on the young child were the Convention on the Rights of the Child, the World Conference on Education for All and the World Summit for Children. The Convention on the Rights of the Child (1991) currently ratified by 127 countries, including India promoted the value of the family, the principles of joint and shared parental responsibilities and the defence of children's rights within a context of gender equality. The World

Conference on Education for All (1990) laid stress on the fact that learning began from birth and pointed out the need for expansion of services for young children, particularly for the disadvantaged and disabled, while the third event, the World Summit for Children (WCEFA 1990), made a plea to the countries to make adequate investment in programmes for child development and education.

These international events made their impact on the national scene too. The Plan of Action (POA) 1992 contained a separate write-up on ECCE and spelled out the details of the future plans in the area. The National Policy on Education (1986), on which the Plan of Action 1992 was based, viewed ECCE as a human resource development programme as well as a feeder and support programme for primary education and as a support service for working women of the disadvantaged sections of the society. While pointing out that the Integrated Child Development Services (ICDS) was the major national scheme for pre-school children, the POA also stressed the need to experiment with more innovative models such as the home-based programme, family day-care centres, etc. The other aspects which were highlighted in the POA was the content and process of ECCE, the training of personnel and monitoring and evaluation.

Apart from the preparation of POA, the other major events in the national scene in ECCE included taking up experimental studies in alternative models of ECCE such as home-based programmes, using educational technology (radio) for fostering child development, family day-care centres, etc. This period also witnessed the development and try-out of a variety of materials for children, teachers and teacher-educators under the NCERT's Project Early Childhood Education/Child Media Laboratory (ECE/CML) in different languages. The other Important events during the period under review were the initiation of a national evaluation study of ICDS by NIPCCD, an impact study of ECE on retention of children in the primary classes by the NCERT, evolving a scheme for monitoring of the pre-school education component in ICDS by NIPCCD, development of a simple tool for assessing early child development by the National Institute of Nutrition (a WHO-ICMR study) and development of a simple tool for screening for mental retardation by the National Institute for the Mentally Handicapped. All these were research studies, which resulted in a better understanding of the impact of ECCE programmes.

The purpose of this brief introduction was to acquaint the reader with the major highlights in the ECCE scene during 1988-92.

The focus of Interest has been on impact and Intervention studies. This is only to be expected as during the period under review, i.e. period of five years 1988-92. The programmes for pre-school children, particularly ICDS, have been stepped up considerably and many researchers got Interested in either examining the impact of the programme or studying the effect of special intervention programmes on Anganwadi children. So the trend seen from 1981 continues in the present period, also. In the other areas, too, the trend is the same, namely in status studies, developmental aspects and training of personnel. Some new areas which emerged in the present period are programme evaluation, adult-child interaction and attitudes, alternate models and establishing the essentials for a pre-school. The new area, programme evaluation, needs to be noted. The large expansion of ICDS programme demanded an evaluation of what it does to the beneficiaries and it is in the fitness of things that a fair amount of studies have been reported in this area. No study has been reported on handicapped children, parent and community involvement and assessment of children. It is however possible that these studies got included under other themes and therefore got omitted from this chapter. As stated earlier the attempts of the National Institute of Nutrition in collaboration with ICMR-WHO in developing a simple screening tool for the psycho-social development of pre-school children and the attempts of the National Institute for the Mentally Handicapped in developing a tool to screen for mental retardation, were noteworthy during the period under survey. Similarly, a good deal of monitoring tools were developed by the National Institute of Public Cooperation and Child Development (NIPCCD) for purposes of monitoring the pre-school education component in the ICDS programme. The NCERT tool developed a whole set of monitoring tools for monitoring the ECE project at the State levels. Many of these tests/tools have found their place in the International survey that was conducted by UNICEF.

2.1 Brief History of Pre-primary Education in India

In our country 'organized education of the child below primary school age did not, until very recently, receive the attention it deserved.

The concept of pre-primary schools was introduced in India by the British missionaries in the latter part of the 18th century when such schools were set up in the western and southern regions of India. Some institutions for training teachers of infant schools were also started by these missionaries.

Mahatma Gandhi's scheme for pre-basic education formulated in the late thirties was the first indigenous scheme for education of very young children and several education reformers and social workers endeavoured to put it into action at the field level Jugartambhai Dave, Nanabhai Bhatt and Tarabai Modak were some of the early pioneers of the every childhood education movement in our country. They were all inspired by the down-to-earth, grassroots level approach of Mahatma Gandhi's pre-basic-education scheme.

The most dominant influence that can be felt even today, as one surveys the contemporary Indian education scene, particularly with reference to early childhood education, is that of Madam Maria Montessori who came to India in 1939 as a refugee from the Fascist regime in Italy. Annnie Besant, a Theosopist, was powerfully influenced by Madam Montessori and she and Rukmini Arundale helped Madam Montessori set up a teacher training centre at Adyar, near Madras. Many early childhood education received their training under Madam Montessori at Adyar and then went over to various parts of the country' and spread the movement for early childhood education. Gujubhai Badheka and Tarabai Modak were among the early educators Who, inspired by Madam Montessori, adapted her methods to suit Indian conditions. They set up the Nutan Bal Shikshan Sangh in 1925. A training center at Bhavanagar Dakshinamoorti was started by Gujubhai and, later, one was set up by Tarabai at Dadar, Bombay. The movement took strong roots in the Suarashtra region of the then province, and also in Madhya Bharat and the Vidarbha region. The early pioneers attempted to develop un indegenous educational system, imbibing the basic Gandhian philosophy and integrating it with the educational principles and scientific pedagogy of Madam Montessori.

During the pre-independence period all these efforts were confined to the voluntary sector and received no support from the government. It was for the first time that, in 1994, a government document, popularly known as the Sargent Committee Report, emphasized the importance of pre-primary education and linked it with the child's educational performance in primarv school. The report viewed pre-primary education as a necessary adjunct to primary education.

During the post-independence period, the movement for the education of young children drew great support from the private and voluntary sectors. Apart from its education values, the 'welfare' dimension also gained recognition. The country's Five Year National Plans, while paying lip service to the need and importance to early childhood education suggested no definite plan or policy in this behalf nor did it make substantial allocations for promoting this field. Many committees and commissions were appointed, both in the education were made for the implementation of the recommendation fo these committees.

It was in the Fifth Five Year Plan that the provision of an integrated package of essential services to young children and pregnant and lactating mothers was conceived and the integrated

Child Development Scheme (ICDS) was launched in 1975 with 66 pilot projects. The ICDS is broadly conceived as an integrated intervention strategy for the holistic development of the young child in the wider context of the family and the larger social group in which the child lives. The integrated packages of service, of which non-formal pre-school education is a component, is delivered through the anganwadi (countryard school) by an anganwadi worker who is picked from the community and given a three-month training. ICDS is currently the biggest programme of early childhood development. It has demonstrated that even a modest investment in child development goes a long way in developing human resources.

The National Policy on Education (1986) has given a great deal of importance to early childhood care and education (ECCE). It views ECCE as an important input in the strategy of human resources development, as a feeder and support programme for primary education and as a support service for working women of the dis-advantaged section of society. (National Policy of Education, 1986, p.2)

In the process of planning and formulating policies related to ECCE, one major drawback that one faces is the lack of a well developed body of research in this field. It is only in the last two decades that researchers from various disciplines have become interested in studying the young child's growth development and learning process. Unlike in the west, where the young child has attracted the attention of anthoropolgists, physchilogists, education, nutritionists, linguists etc, who have studied the child from their respective perspectives, in India the young child as a subject of research has been neglected. The little research that is available today is scattered piecemeal and in small watertight compartments. This would become evident as one reviews the researches conducted in the field over the last 30 to 35 years.

2. 2 History, Need and Status Studies

Five studies are reported in this area, all of which are status studies. Three of these studies are state-level studies: Maiyani,

J.P.'s (1989) study on development of pre-primary education in Gujarat from a historical perspective, PankaJam, G. et al.'s (1990a) study on child-care services in Tamil Nadu and Rajalakshami, M.'s (1992) study of the assessment of nursery education in Kerala. The other two are city studies, Mishra. D.'s (1990) study of the problems of pre-school education in Cuttack city and Sharma R.'s (1992) comparative study of aided and unaided pre-schools of Pune city.

The quality of these studies vary, some being rambling and unfocused, while others had a sharper focus. The study in Gujarat came to the conclusion that despite quantitative expansion of pre-school education, the present set-up was not satisfactory in terms of curriculum and teacher training, while the study in Kerala pointed out that physical facilities needed to be improved and a more uniform curriculum needed to be introduced. The study in Tamil Nadu however showed that the child-care services of children in the age-group of 2-5 years were impressive, as the State had achieved a minimum level of provision for all children; the State now needed to pay more attention to the under twos and also to improving the quality of training of the child-care workers.

Both the city studies found a prevailing over-emphasis on formal learning and evaluation and emphasised the need to introduce more play-way methods. Small-sample studies undertaken inn other cities like Delhi, Bombay, Hyderabad, Chandigarh, Bangalore, etc. have also shown that pre-schools are run as mere downward extensions of primary schools and that children are under pressure to cope with formal skills such as reading, writing and number work. The situation is grave and it needs to be looked into on a priority basis. The report of the Yashpal Committee has spelled out the trauma that the children are facing. Steps are being taken by the NCERT as well as the professional organizations like the Indian Association for Pre-School Education (IAPE) as well as organization Mondiale Pour L'Education Prescolaire (OMEP) (The World Organisation for Early Childhood Education) to place the issues before the schools and to convince them about the necessity to introduce play- and activity-based learning in the pre-schools. A fair amount of success has been achieved in getting schools to do away with admission tests for children and getting them to use alternate methods for screening. There is still a long way to go but a beginning has been made in this direction.

2.3 Developmental Aspects and Personality

Three studies are reported in the areas of developmental aspects and personality traits. These include a study of behaviour problems of pre-school children and the effect of behaviour modification techniques on aggressive pre-school children attending Anganwadi centres in Chandigarh by Devl, B. (1990): Murthy, V.'s (1992) investigation into the scholastic readiness of pre-school children of Bombay: and Singh. A.'s (1987) study of language development of , two- to three-year old children of Allahabad. As evident, the studies conducted in these areas are limited in number. They focused on different aspects of development and therefore no common trend can be elicited. It is obvious that more studies need to be taken up to study aspects such as cognitive development, particularly in thinking and reasoning skills, memory, etc., and in social development including leadership skills, beginnings of prejudice, etc. The play is another area where more information is required. The play patterns pre-school children, gender difference in play, play and its effect on the personality development of children, etc., need to be looked into. We also need more in-depth studies on specific groups of children such as tribal children, bilingual and multilingual children slum children etc. How deprivation and malnourishment affect the pre-schooler's development is another area that needs to be studied more systematically.

2.4 Training of Personnel

Only two studies are reported in this area. One by Khosla, R. (1991) on the evaluation of the refresher course in pre-school education for the Anganwadi workers, and the other by Muralidharan, R. and Pankajam, G. (1988) on evaluation of different models of pre-school teacher training from the point of view of their impact on children. Both studies were methodologically sound and answered questions that are relevant to pre-school teacher education. Khosla, R.'s (1991) study showed that refresher training in pre-school education was beneficial to Anganwadi workers both in terms of organising activities for children as well as in Involving the helpers and mothers in the programme. In spite of such findings, it was later decided by the administrators to do away with the specialized course in pre-school education and introduce a more generalised refresher course. Such decisions make one wonder about the usefulness and scope of such evaluative studies. The second study may be looked at from a historical perspective. Tamil Nadu is a state which has a long history In pre-school education as well as pre-school teacher education. The state experimented with different models of pre-school teacher training and it was appropriate to look into the effectiveness of these models, primarily from the point of view of children's development.

It does not stand to reason why only two studies are reported in this important area, considering the fact that the quality of pre-school education depends primarily on the strength of the teachers. It is obvious that this area is a totally neglected one. More studies need to be conducted on teacher training, particularly from the point of curriculum, training methodology and the competence of the teacher educators. The country offers differs models of ECCE pre-service training at different levels beginning from grass-roots-level training of Anganwadi workers to the postgraduate diploma in ECCE. In addition, many institutions conduct In-service training. There are also models of distance training in ECCE being followed in the country. It is therefore important that methodologically sound studies are conducted in this area so that more meaningful information will be available.

2.5 Studies on Impact and International and Programme Evaluation

The maximum number of studies have been reported in this category. Due to the rapid expansion of pre-school programmes like the ICDS, many researchers probably got interested in this type of research as it gave them a ready-made laboratory for either intervening or for measuring impact. Nine impact studies and five intervention studies have been reported during this period.

As regards the impact studies, they are varied in nature, some studied the impact of pre-school experience right at the pre-school stage itself while others studied the Impact at the primary school stage, and a third type traced the impact right up to the pre-adolescent and adolescent stage. Except for Chandrika, D.C.'s (1989) study, all other studies showed a positive impact, while Chandrika found no difference between children who had the Anganwadi experience and those who did not have such experience, with reference to their cognitive development at 6-7 years of age, in Tirupati. A study the one out in this group of impact studies, is that done by Kaul, V. et al (1992) on retention in primary schools. It is a tracer study done in different States on underprivileged tribal and rural children who had pre-school experience of fairly good quality. It was seen that good quality pre-school experience led to improvement of the retention rate at the primary stage. This study is significant particularly at this stage when the country is struggling to meet the .target of universal elementary education. Another study which was also a follow-up study was by Muralidharan, R. et al. (1992) on the children of Bastar. These children had some enriched Anganwadi experience about ten years ago and the study attempted to trace these children to see how they were faring in the primary, school. It showed that approximately 50% of children was attending the primary school but only 30% were in the right classes. The quality of learning was also found to be low. The other studies which measured the impact of pre-school experience at the primary stage were those done by Mandke. S. (1989) and Pattanaik, A. (1991). Mandke, S. (1989) examined the learning readiness of Class I children while Pattanaik, A. (1991) studied the cognitive development of children In Classes I to III. While Pattaniak, A.(1991) and Mandke, S.(1989) got positive results. Pattanaik. A.'s (1991) study yielded results in favour of pre-schooled children in only ten out of twenty-six tasks.

The two studies which looked into the impact at the pre-adolescent and adolescent stages were by Tripathy, A. (1991) and Jachuk, K. (1990), both studying cognitive development. Both are more or less similar studies done in Bhubaneshwar yielding the finding that pre-school experience helped in developing the cognitive abilities of children and that the influence was long-term and persisted upto the adolescent stage.

Pandey, H. (1989) also studied the impact of f pre-school experience on the cognitive development of children but she concentrated at the pre-school stage itself. Pandey. H. (1989) studied children with and without Anganwadi experience, and found that pre-school/Anganwadi experience helped children in their cognitive development.

Thus, by and large, the impact studies showed that pre-school experience helped children in their development. However, more studies are required in this category, particularly in areas such as socio-emotional and language development. Well-planned longitudinal studies should throw more light on what early childhood stimulation does to the total development of an individual.

The intervention studies conducted are only six in number. Almost all studies focused on intervention to foster cognitive components in children: Hejmadi, A.'s (1991) study on intelligence and creativity, Manju, Vani E.'s (1986) study on perception. Mishra, S.'s (1991a) on intelligence and curiosity. Srivastava. S.'s (1992) on concept formation and language development. Kaul. V. et al.'s. (1992) on number readiness and Subhashini. T.'s (1990) on readiness in reading, writing and arithmetic. All studies except that of Srivastava. S. (1992) and perhaps to some extent that of Subhashini, T. (1990) were done on small samples and each of them proved the effectivèness of intervention for fostering specific developments in children. Srivastava. S.'s (1992) study had a larger sample drawn from different types of pre-schools. She introduced science-oriented educational toys into the pre-school programme and studied their effect on concept formation in children. No study was reported on any aspect other than cognitive development. What kinds of Intervention are required in fostering socio-emotional aspects of development, is a question that is yet to be answered.

Next to impact and intervention studies, come the programme evaluation studies. Eight such studies were reported, six of which pertained to ICDS. The major studies in this category were undertaken by NIPCCD. The national evaluation of ICDS was an important hallmark which yielded some good insights into the functioning of this giant programme. It was a mammoth study, the sample consisting of 100 ICDS projects from 98 districts spaced over 54 rural, 28 tribal and 18 urban projects: from each project seven Anganwadis were selected at random. The study used four schedules, for households, beneficiaries, community leaders and functionaries. Some of the major findings were that while the positive impact of ICDS was visible in terms of health, nutrition and education of children, there was a need to upgrade physical infrastructural facilities of Anganwadis, to strengthen the training of the functionaries, to improve pre-school education by providing appropriate aids and materials and to strengthen the components of community participation.

The next important study was Sood, N.'s (1987) Appraisal of Pre-school Education in ICDS. Infact the other studies. Mistry, V.: Kaul, S. and Dhar, H.'s (1989) In-depth study of Baroda urban block and Sood, N.'s (1987) evaluation of Mangolpuri block form parts of this total appraisal. In addition, the appraisal study was done In three more projects: Jama Masjid, Junna and Coimbatore. This study was taken up with the aim of developing a system of monitoring the social components of ICDS and following a common research design. From each project, 64 children In the age-group of 3-6 years drawn from the highest-ranking Anganwadi (HRA) and the lowest-ranking Anganwadi (LRA) formed the ICDS sample while a matched group of a minimum of 10 children with no exposure to pre-school education formed the non-ICDS sample. The mothers of all these children were also included in the sample. In addition, a sample of 40 children who had Anganwadi experience and were at present enrolled in Classes I and II and a matching group of 20 children studying In Classes I and II but without any Anganwadi experience were also studied in each project. The pre-school children were developmentally assessed while the primary school children were assessed through rating by their teachers, and mothers' awareness was assessed by Interview schedules. Some of the major findings were that while the overall developmental status of ICDS group was superior to that of the non-ICDS children, the superior performance of the HRA groups as compared to that of the LRA group showed that it was not the mere exposure to Anganwadi but the quality of Input which was important in bringing about a significant raise in the developmental status of children. This study is an example of how collaborating institutions can pursue a study following a common research design, yet giving each collaborator freedom to put the extra Inputs If desired. For a large country like India, such studies-involving inter-centre collaboration, are vital as such collaboration yields more reliable and meaningful results.

The next study on ICDS is a study to establish a monitoring system, undertaken by Sharma, A. (1992) In the districts of Bhiwani and Adampur in Haryana. It showed the need to integrate information regarding all aspects of ICDS at one place to give a holistic picture of ICDS implementation.

The other two studies, one by Muralldharan, R. and Upadhyay, G.C. (1992) on an evaluation of Toy Making Competition for pre-school and primary school teachers and the other by Rawal, U. (1992) on programme evaluation of a model remedial pre-school are outside the ICDS context. The first one through questionnaires distributed to prize-winning teachers and their heads of schools and Field Advisors of the NCERT who conducted these competitions at the state-levels showed that the involvement of the district-level staff was absolutely vital for the success of the programme. Rawal, U.'s (1992) study is different from all other studies as it restricted itself to the programme evaluation of one single school and as such is not comparable to the other studies in this category.

It is heartening to see the trend of setting up studies for programme evaluation. With the expansion of child-care programmes, such studies should prove useful in helping the policy planners to gain insights; into the effectiveness of different types of programmes.

2.6 Studies on Alternate Models and on Establishing the Essentials

The studies reported in this category are one by Muralidharan, R. and Mishra, S. (1989) on developing a home-based model and the other by Dutta, V. (1992) on family day-care centres. The POA (1992) had pointed out the necessity to take up more studies in developing alternate models of ECCE primarily with the aim of expanding ECCE services. The study of Muralldharan, R. and Mishra. S. (1989) followed an experimental-control design with a fairly long period of a one-year Intervention for the experimental group. They showed that given training, the uneducated, unskilled tribal mothers were in a position to function as educators of their pre-school children but the intervention did not prove effective in the case of the mothers of urban slums. The sample consisted of 65 tribal families and 160 urban slum homes and the measuring instruments used were developmental tests for children and interview schedules for mothers.

Dutta, V. 's (1992) is a comparative study of family day-care centres and regular day-care centres of Bombay. Her sample consisted of 80 children each from family day-care and regular day-care centres. 40 from low-quality centers and 40 from high quality centres. She used tools such as day-care centre environment rating scales, Interview guide for care givers and questionnaires for parents. Some of the major findings were that there was an edge in favour of family day-care centres, particularly in terms of hygiene and meal-time routines, and also that the group size has an Impact on the quality of the centers.

More studies in this category are warranted, particularly In terms of training of the care givers, supervision and monitoring of such centres, specifying minimum essential requirements for running such centres, etc.

Two studies are reported in this category but the studies are of a totally different nature. The empirical study of Nagalakshml, J. (1991) aimed to study the effects of group size. space and play equipment and staff-child ratios on behaviour of children and thereby arrive at an "ideal" requirement for pre-schools. Nagalakshmi's sample of schools was drawn from three different towns of Andhra Pradesh and Included 529 schools in all. She used time sampling technique in conducting the observation and combined it with personal enquiry. The study arrived at general recommendations such as the need for encouraging active play and cooperative play, making provision for adequate play equipment, improving staff-child ratio, etc.

The other study in this category was by Seth, K. and Ahuja, K. (1992) of the NCERT on establishing minimum specifications for pre- schools. The aim of this study was to specify the essential and desirable prerequisites for a quality pre-school programme, keeping in view the contextual realities of the country. The method followed was to prepare the draft document and present it in a series of workshops to experts in the field so as to finalise it and circulate it all over the country. The document spelled out the requirements in terms of physical facilities, equipment and material, safety precautions, the pre-school staff, age for admission, admission procedure, pre-school programme and records and registers. This is a useful document which needs to be tried out in different contexts, primarily with the objective to see whether a quality programme can be ensured if the given prerequisites are fulfilled. It should also serve as a good tool for monitoring pre-school programmes. It was in the fitness of things that the Indian Association for Pre-School Education (IAPE) reprinted the document in its bulletin *Balak* so as to bring it to the notice of pre-school workers all over the country.

2.7 Studies on Ecce Personnel

Two studies were reported in this category, both from Tirupati and both dealing with Anganwadi workers. While Geetha, K. (1990)

studied the knowledge and competence of the Anganwadi workers (AWWs). Kumari, P. (1991) dealt with their job involvement, personality and performance. Geeta. K.'s (1990) sample consisted of 45 Anganwadi workers who attended a monthly meeting of the urban ICDS block in Tirupati. The tools used were questionnaires to assess knowledge and competence of the Anganwadi workers. The major findings were that almost all the Anganwadi workers had above seventy-five per cent knowledge in the areas of ICDS and 80% of them were found to be highly competent. This of course speaks well for the project of Tirupati but the methodology of using a questionnaire to assess the competence of the workers was certainly not a good choice.

Kumari, P.'s (1991) study was more detailed and was done on a sample of 115 Anganwadi workers belonging to both urban and rural centres, 8 supervisors and 345 beneficiaries. The tools used were a job involvement scale, a work involvement scale, a job stress scale and rating scales to assess job performance. Urban and rural differences were highlighted in the study, the urban Anganwadi workers showing better job and work involvement and experiencing less job stress.

More studies may be planned to examine he competence level of the child-care worker. The personality characteristics of a highly competent worker and the possible reasons that enable her to function effectively. The system employs different types of workers, ranging from semi-literate to highly qualified women, working differing contexts. Questions such as whether there is a common denominator for job satisfaction and competence irrespective of context and qualifications of the workers, needs to be probed.

2.8 Studies on Adult-Chile-Interaction and Attitudes of Adults

Four studies were reported in this category, three on adult-child interaction and one on attitudes of parents and teachers on various aspects of pre-school education. Seth, P. (1991): Srilatha,

G. (1988) and Bagai, R. (1988), probed into the Implications of adult-child interaction for children's growth while Yasodhara, P. (1991) examined the attitudes of parents and teachers towards pre-school education. Bagai, R.'s (1988) study is interesting as she made detailed observations of adult-child interaction in three different communities, with the aim to understand the family dynamics of some of the Indian sub-cultures in relation to the developmental status of young children of 1-7 years. Seth, P. (1991), on the other hand, made a psychometric study on 240 children using a child-competence scale thereby selecting 30 children each at the two ends of the competence continuum and then studying the interaction of parents with these children by using an interview schedule. Srilatha, G. (1988) studied 300 mothers of pre-school children from different socio-economic groups using an, interview schedule on mother-child interaction, primarily focusing on SES and sex differences in interaction.

Yasodhara, P.'s (1991) work pertained to a study of the attitude of parents and teachers with regard to the objectives and curriculum of pre-school education and the priority groups of children in need of pre-schooling. Yasodhara used questionnaires for parents and teachers and she found that there was a need to educate them as they did not have a clear idea regarding the purpose of pre-school education and their role in the children's life.

The interaction studies need to be improved considerably. Highly sophisticated research methodology is now being used in international research on mother-child interactions. Video recording of the interactions and subsequent detailed analysis of the interaction, is an example. What is important in such studies is to place the study in the right theoretical framework, to make detailed observations, to ensure that objectivity is maintained in the interpretation, etc. Adult-child interaction across different subcultures also needs to be probed. Gender differences in interactions, interactions with grandparents, etc., are also topics for further study.

Miscellaneous Studies

Two studies are placed in this category as they were very different from all other studies. Deepali, D.'s (1990) study on pre-school children and their problems .n rural areas of Kamrup district is mostly sociological in nature and deals with problems such as alcoholism of men, tension between mother-in-law and daughter-in-law, etc. Probably the attempt was to link it with pre-school problems but this is not very clear.

The other is a review by Mohite, P. (1990) of researches In ECCE, a trend report.

After giving a brief picture of ECCI researches at the national level, it may perhaps be useful be useful to give a bird's eye view of what happened at the international level in ECCE during the period under consideration.

2.9 The International Research Working on Early Childhood Education

The *International Encyclopedia of Education* reported three waves of research on child-care and pre-school education (Crahay, M. 1994). The first wave primarily consisted of American researches studying the effects of pre-school education, many of which yielded the finding that pre-school intervention could have lasting positive effects. The second wave of studies focused on comparative evaluation of the different models of pre-school programmes but these studies did not yield any conclusive evidence. Presently, the contemporary third wave studies therefore try to find an answer to what really happens in different child-care and school settings. The evidence is slowly accumulating to the effect that pre-school intervention helps in fostering child development but the multiple and complex factors that Influence It may vary from one context to the other. What emerges is that interaction of pre-school Intervention with the other social contextual factors in the child's world needs to be kept In view while the attempts are made to measure the Impact of pre-school education. An Interactive ecological research framework is therefore desirable and a shift is slowly being indicated from the "currently dominant process-product paradigm to an ecological mediating process framework", (p. 687)

Kamerman, S.B. (1994) indicated in international overview of Child Care Policies and Programmes that all European countries were moving towards universal coverage of pre-school children in the 3-6 years age-group through publicly funded programmes focusing of developmentally appropriate programming. These countries view early childhood education as a public responsibility and as an entitlement for children, and efforts are being stepped up to expand the programme to cover the whole cohort. Yet quality differences in terms of group size. adult-child ratio, staff qualifications, etc., do exist between countries. A growing trend is also seen to ensure safe infant-care for the under threes by extending parenting leave it some form or the other.

Myers. R.G. (1988) showed by reviewing Latin American and Asian studies that early childhood provision helped to address social equality issues. Early intervention programmes showed a positive effect on primary school enrolment, initial adjustment and on achievement in the early years of primary school achievement in the early years primary school Myers, R.G. and Hertenberg. R. (1987) found that the value of early childhood programming went far beyond the children and extended to the care givers and community. It was, therefore, important that early childhood programming should not be done in isolation from programming for the other. Engle, P. (1986), in a research review discovered that variables such as mother's positive self-image, knowledge of the culture and practical know-how contribute to the child's well-being.

The 1990s are therefore the era for building programmes from family strengths. Yet more information is required on what provisions should be made and which sectors of the community should be involved, and on the nature of programming.

Another area which is a matter of great the concern in the International research scene is the area of assessment of young children. Young era children by their very nature have certain limitations. These include their restricted ability to comprehend assessment cues, their limited information-processing, verbal and perceptual-motor skills and their difficulty in controlling their behaviour during the assessment sessions. Due to these complexities a mixed measurement strategy is warranted In early childhood that incorporates multiple Indicators and multiple sources of Information. Assessment in early childhood is highly context-specific and inferential In character (Meisels, S.J. 1994). It has to view the child from multiple perspectives rather than rely on isolated single sources of information. The principle of contextualisation appears to be the all important principle in early childhood assessment as the child's performance depends to a great extent on the context in which a task is presented. Guidelines for screening and assessing young children are now available in the recent research literature (Meisels, S.J. 1987. 1989a. 1989b and Meisels, S.J. and Provence, S. 1989). Meisels, S.J. and Provence. S. (1989) listed 41 different areas of early childhood development screening tests, general development inventories, cognitive assessment devices, communication assessment instruments, motor assessment devices, social/emotional assessments and self-help assessment Instruments.

What is on now is the search for development predictors. Long-term predictability of early childhood assessment scores needs to be considerably improved. Probably a longitudinal, multivariate design may help us better to understand which variables sampled in which specific ways, at which particular points of time, differentiate between poor and high achievers at later stages of development.

2.10 Conclusion

To conclude, research interest in the area of ECCE has certainly increased but studies more inter-disciplinary in nature are required, particularly to understand the effects of multiple factors on child development. Also, more investigations need to be taken up to examine the long-term effects of ECCE on children.

Well-designed longitudinal studies are what we require at the moment. Personnel preparation is another area that deserves more attention. Different models of personnel preparation exist now in ECCE but no research evidence is available on the effect of these models. Similarly, we require more information regarding ECCE in different specific contexts such as tribal areas, urban slums. Hence, the selection of the topic "The working of Balawadee Centers in Twin Cities of Hyderabad and Secunderabad- A critical study of the opinions of Community members and parents".

3

Research Procedures and Methodology

The present chapter states the design of the study and provides a description of the research procedure. It includes the statement of the problem, the objectives of the study identification of variables, formulation of hypotheses, description of tools, statistical techniques used and operational definitions of concepts and organization of the study.

3.1 Statement of the Problem

"The Working of Balawadees in Twin Cities of Hyderabad and Secunderabad: A Critical Study of the Opinion of Community Members and Parents."

The study of Balawadee Centers caters to the educational needs of 3 to 6 years age group of children living in urban slums of twin cities of Hyderabad and Secunderabad. This study is important as there is need for developing the system of early childhood education particularly in urban slum areas since, almost all the women go to work and also since the home and community situations are not congenial for the healthy growth of children. Further, the educational, health, and nutritional services are not effectively reaching the slum children. Organizing pre-school activity will help the children of disadvantaged sections in reaching the educational, health and other welfare services effectively. There is need to study the pre-primary education status of slum dwellers as they constitute a significant percentage of population.

This study is a descriptive research, it finds out the existing position of 20 Balawadees located in Hyderabad and Secunderabad, popularly known as twin cities. This study will probe into the opinion of and the experiences of parents of the children who are studying in these Balawadees, the opinions of community members residing in the viscinity of Balawdees.

3.2 Objectives of the Study

1. To find out and assess the opinions of community members and parents on the infrastructure facilities available under the Urban Community Development Educational Programme. (UCDEP)
2. To find out the opinions of community members and parents about the health care facilities of Balawadees under UCDEP.
3. To enquire into the opinions of community members and parents on the suitablity of the curriculum of Balawadee centers under UCDEP.
4. To study the opinions of community members and parents on monitoring pattern followed in Balawadee centers under UCDEP.
5. To study the opinions of community members and parents on Quality of Infrastructural facilities available in Balawadees under UCDEP.
6. To understand the opinions of community members and parents on Teacher participation existing under Balawadee System of UCDEP.
7. To find out the opinions of community members and parents on Learning Environment existing in Balawadees under UCDEP.

3.3 Description of Variables

To study the early childhood education in the Balawadees existing in slums of Hyderabad and Secunderabad survey method

Figure - 3.1 Graphic Design of the Study

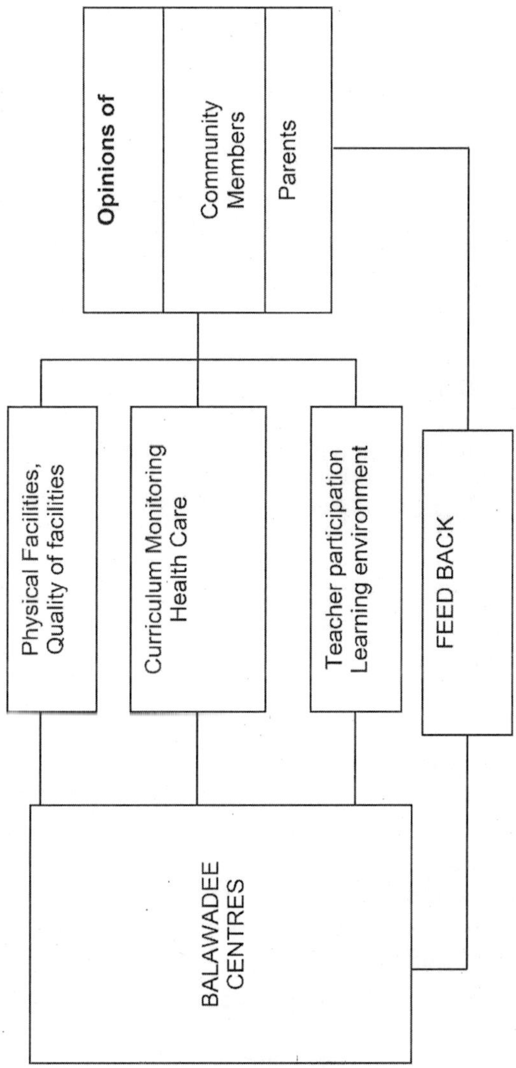

is employed. In order to identify the areas to be covered by the opinionnaire the researcher has reviewed the related literature available related to the problem under study. In view of the suggestions of the experts the researcher has identified the following areas of study on working of Balawadee centers. The major dependent variables under study are:

(1) The Availability of infrastructure facilities in the Balawadee centers
(2) Health Care facilities available
(3) Curriculum suitability
(4) Monitoring of Balawadees
(5) The Quality of Infrastructure facilities existing in Balawadees
(6) Teacher participation under Balawadee system
(7) Learning Environment existing in the Balawadee system.

The independent variables under study are as follows:

(1) Age
(2) Gender
(3) Caste
(4) Religion
(5) Education
(6) Income
(7) Occupation

3.4 Hypotheses

Corresponding to the objectives stated, the following hypotheses are formulated.

(i) There is no association between the opinions of community members and parents on infrastructural facilities existing and the attributes of respondents like age, gender, caste, religion, education, income and occupation

(ii) There is no association between the opinions of community members and parents on Healthcare facilities in the Balawadees and the age, gender caste, religion, education, income and occupational facts of the respondents.

(iii) There is no association between the opinions of community members and parents on Curriculum Contents followed and the different attributes of respondents like age, gender, caste, religion, education, income and occupational qualities of the respondents.

iv) There is no association between opinions of community members and parents on monitoring pattern followed in and the attributes of respondents like age, gender, caste, religion, education, income and occupational.

v) There is no association between opinions of community members and parents on the quality of infrastructural facilities existing in different Balawadees and the age, gender, caste, religion, education, income and occupational qualities of the respondents.

vi) There is no association between opinions of community members and parents on teacher participation in the Balawadees schools and the attributes of respondents like age, gender, caste, religion, education, income and occupational qualities.

vii) There is no association between opinions of community members and parents on learning environment existing in Balawadee Pre-primary schools and the age, gender, caste, religion, education, income and occupational facts of the respondents.

3.5 Description of Tools and Standardisation

After the review of related literature and having consulted the experts, the officials of UCDEP a base line survey was conducted with the help of a questionnarie (appendix III) this questioner contained four parts I, II, III and IV. With the help of this questionnaire discussions were held with fifteen teachers of Balawadees fifty parents and fifty community members in the viscientity of twenty balawadee centers under study. Based on the insights gained and knowledge of the status of the balawadees a detailed opinionnaire was prepared. This opinionnaire (Appendix I) served as the main tool of the investigation.

In other words to realize the objectives identified and to test hypotheses formulated a tool has been constructed to critically study the opinions of community members and parents of children about functioning of Balawadees.

In the first phase of the development of the tool, certain important dimensions of the study have been identified. Experts opinions were also collected in the identifications of the dependent variables. The following dependent variables were finally selected.

1. The availability of infrastructural facilities in Balawadee centers.
2. Health care facilities available in Balawadees.
3. Curriculum suitability
4. Monitoring on Balawadees
5. The quality of infrastrutural facilities existing in Balwadees
6. Teacher participation under Balawadee system
7. Learning Environment existing in the Balawadee system.

Under each dimension a set of closed items were prepared with the ratings low, medium and high, to capture the correct opinions of the respondents. The preliminary draft was submitted to a panel of experts for identifying the items relevance, suitability of answering the research questions and representiveness. The final items selected by the experts are considered to be having content validity and conceptual validity.

The scoring procedures adopted to analyse the opinions of the respondents were also finalized by taking the opinions of experts depending on the level of precisions with respect to the correct opinion. The responses were categorized into three groups:

1. Low
2. Medium
3. High

And accordingly first, second and third scores were assigned.

The tool prepared by the above process was administered on a sample of 30 community members and 30 parents and they were asked to express their opinions according to the instructions provided. Further, the tool was administered strictly by taking all the precausions. During the process of this phase of study the researcher clarified the doubts raised by the respondents regarding various items. After a gap of one month, the tool was readministered on the same sample i.e., 30 community members and thirty parents and the opinions were recoded and analysed. Scores obtained in both the cases were used to obtain reliability co-efficeint i.e., the co-efficient of co-relation was computed by using Pearson Product Movement Co-relation. The reliablility of the tool can be expressed in terms of Standard Error of Measurement. It is said that for the purpose of interpreting the individual scores the standard of measurement is more useful then reliability co-efficeint. Therefore, the researcher computed the standard error of measurement by using the formula.

$$\text{Means} = SD_1\sqrt{1-r_{11}}$$

Where SD_1 is the standard deviation of the scores in the first case and r_{11} is the reliability co-efficient of the tool. The following table represents the reliability co-efficient, the reliability index and also the proporation of error component.

The above table indicates that the proportion of error component is less and hence the tool satisfies the consistency of scores and therefore, it is reliable.

Further, Garette (1979) suggested that the reliability indices of the test can also sometimes be taken as measures of validity. He considers that the test with reliability indices of 0.5 or less are extremently poor. But to conclude that the tools constructed in this study are valid. Also, it is mentioned that the experts in the field of education judged the adequacy of the content. In order to recheck the content validity of the tools responses were collected on each item in two phases and these cases were co-related, by using the

Table 3.1 : Showing the reliability co-effiencent, reliability index and proportion of error component, between each of dependent variable mentioned under column area with the seven independent variables i.e., Age, Gender, Caste, Religion, Education, Income and Occupation.

S.No.	*Area*	*Reliability co-efficient*	*Reliability Index*	*Proportion of Error components*
1.	Infrastructural facilities	0.63	0.783	0.37
2.	Health Care	0.66	0.823	.034
3.	Curriculum Suitability	0.72	0.878	0.29
4.	Monitoring on Balawadees	0.63	0.873	0.37
5.	Quality of Infrastructure	0.65	0.821	0.34
6.	Teacher Participation	0.72	0878	.29
7.	Learning Environment	0.71	0.876	0.28

scale developed by Vasilios Kauliadis and Job Ogborn. The co-efficient of correlation between scores for all the items were found to be above 0.69, which shows the validity of the items of the opinionnarie. In the final stage of the development of the tool, the results obtained in the pilot study were seriously considered on the basis of these results and also on the reliability and validity measures. By following these procedures the final form of the tool was prepared.

Anatomy of the Opinionnaire

The opinionnaire comprises two parts, viz. part A and part B. The opinionnaire was pre-tested and the items were modified with the consultation of experts, before administering on the sample. It contains carefully constructed them along with covering letter from the researcher explaining the purpose of the study. It assured the respondent that delicate information will be held in strict confidence.

Part A Personal Data

This is meant to gather personal information of the respondents, the parents and the community members part A includes name, sex, religion, caste, education income level and occupational level of the respondents.

Part B : Contains the statements on a 3-points scale related to the following aspects :

Part A. Availability of infrastructural facilities existing in Balawadees

This section comprises of seven question with multiple choice responses on infrastructural and physical facilities and related aspects about which the respondents give out their opinion on a 3-point scale. The infrastructure regarding classrooms, sanitary facilities, electricity connection, seating arrangement, black board, drinking water, toilets, playground, classroom size etc. Open ended questions are also given in the section to explore their opinion towards pre-primary education and related aspects.

Part B : Health Care facilities

In this part the opinions are collected with respect health care facilities which include supply of medical services and medicines given for curative and preventive diseases, supply of nutritious food, first aid facilities and health checkup programmes etc.

Part C: Curriculum Suitability

Under this section the nature and content of curriculum are studied and the curriculum related practices adopted in the Balwadees are also studied.

Part D: Monitoring

Under this section opinions on the monitoring pattern followed was studied from the community members and parents.

Part E : Quality of infrastructure

The quality of infrastructure facilities rated at three levels. They are: (1) low quality/status (2) medium quality/status and (3) high quality/status.

Part F: Teacher participation

In this part opinions of parents and community members are collected about teachers participation related to methods and material adopted in the teaching learning process. An attempt is made to assess the performance of teachers based on the opinions of the parents and community members.

Part G : Learning Environment

Under this section the opinions about the learning environment existing in Balawadees are studied from parents and community members regarding the behaviour of the teacher, rapport maintained by teacher, the commitment of the teacher are studied.

The opinionnaire was prepared in English Medium. It was administered on the sample drawn from Hyderabad and

Secunderabad cities. Wherever necessary Telugu translation of the script was used.

3.6 Selection of Sample

In twin cities of Hyderabad and Secunderabad there are twenty Balawadee Centers. Fifteen are in Hyderabad and Five are in Secunderabad

All the twenty centers have been studied. In selecting the sample from among the parents and community members random sampling method was used.

The sample for the study includes parents and community members educated uneducated, employed and unemployed men and women of Hyderabad and Secunderabad cities in the vicinity of Balawadee Centers. The respondents are drawn from the twin cities from various religious caste and income groups who constitute the major cultural groups in the society. The employment level of the sample include particular specified jobs such as office clerks, officers, daily wage labourers, small vendors, etc.

The sample include men and women of married and unmarried status with different monthly income levels; consists of two categories of people who are associated with the working of Balawadees. They are 1) The parents of the children studying in Balawadees 2) The community members who are local residents staying in the neighborhood rendering social services for the welfare of the people. These members are identified by urban community development for any activities under taken by Balawadees and its effective functioning. The details of the respondents are given below:

A random sampling design was adopted and the opinionnaire was given to 500 parents and 500 community members however the responses which are in full form were selected for detailed analysis and study. The final sample includes 161 opinionnaires from Secunderabad 489 opinionnaires from Hyderabad were finally used for the study (As shown in table 3.2). Most of the opinionnaires

Table 3.2 : Table Showing the Sample Selected for the Study

S.No	*Name of the Balawadee*	*Location*	*Responses of Parents*	*Responses of Community Members*	*Total*
1.	Om Nagar	Hyderabad	22	10	32
2.	Hussaini Bagh	Hyderabad	22	10	32
3.	Chandra Nagar	Hyderabad	22	10	32
4.	Jowahar Nagar	Hyderabad	22	10	32
5.	Bayya Ka Bagh	Hyderabad	22	10	32
6.	Qulinder Nagar	Hyderabad	20	12	32
7.	Anand Nagar	Hyderabad	22	12	34
8.	Gulshan Nagar	Hyderabad	20	12	32
9.	Vette Pally	Hyderabad	20	12	32
10.	Konda Reddy Guda	Hyderabad	22	12	34

(Contd.)

(Contd. Table 3.2)

S.No	*Name of the Balawadee*	*Location*	*Responses of Parents*	*Responses of Community Members*	*Total*
11.	Mahamood Nagar	Hyderabad	22	11	33
12.	Quazi Pura	Hyderabad	22	10	32
13.	Saber Nagar	Hyderabad	22	10	32
14.	Ibrahim Bagh	Hyderabad	22	12	34
15.	Isamiah Bazar	Hyderabad	22	12	34
16.	Achaiah Nagar	Secunderabad	22	12	34
17.	Murad Nagar	Secunderabad	22	10	32
18.	Gayetri Nagar	Secunderabad	20	11	31
19.	Lohia Nagar	Secunderabad	22	11	33
20.	Krishna Nagar	Secunderabad	20	11	31
	TOTAL		430	220	650

were administered personally explaining the purpose of the study and clarifying wherever needed. Some opinionnaires were administered through mail taking enough care of the postages etc.

In total 650 responses from both the cities were taken for this study.

Place	*Parents*	*Community members*	*Total*
Hyderabad	324	165	489
Secunderabad	106	55	161
TOTAL	430	220	650

3.7 Statistical Techniques Used

The data collected was properly coded and verified with the help of a coded design which was prepared exclusively for this purpose. Coded data was entered on separate code-sheet and analyzed using the computer facility. Data was analyzed by means of frequency tabulation.

Item analysis, counting the percentages of each responses to the opinion was carried independently for the respondents of twin cities and also the cumulative analyses of the responses of the respondents put together.

To measure the association between independent variables such as sex, age of the respondent, religion, caste, educational level, occupation, income on the issues under study namely infrastructural facilities, health care facilities, curriculum suitability monitoring, quality of infrastructure facilities, teacher participation and learning environment of Balawadees.

The study applied the percentages and ψ^2 (chi-square) test to estimate the opinions of respondents from varied backgrounds on aspects under the study.

3.8 Operational Definition of Concepts

The following are the *1

1. Early: It refers to age prior to school entry upto age 8

2. Child : Person from conception to age 18 (CRC definition)

3. Care: What family members and other members of society do for a child to facilitate the process of growth and development.

4. Survival: Absence of mortality including health

5. Growth: is an increase in size, which requires food nutrition particularly under the age of two and for women during pregnancy and lactation.

6. Development: Refers to an orderly process along a continuous path, in which a child learns to handle more complicated levels of moving, thinking, speaking, feeling and relating to others. Children vary enormously in their rates of development, but all cover essentially the same sequence of developmental changes.

7. Balawadee Centers: It is an educational Institute for pre-primary education established under matching grants by MCH and UNICEF with co-operation and of Local people, for the Slum dwellers in the twin cities of Hyderabad and Secunderabad. For the age group of 2 to 10 years.

8. Community Members: The active residents of Balawadee area under reference who initiated the idea of establishment of balawadee and who are identified by urban community development department as active members responsible for effective functioning of Balwadees. On an average there are about Twenty such members in each Balwadee Center.

9. Parents: Mother and Father of the students studying in Balawadies Centers.

10. Infrastructure facilities: Refers to minimum requirements in Balawadies such as Classroom furniture, Black board, Seating arrangement, Ventilation, water and toilets facilities.

11. Health Care : The treatment of Curative and Prentive ailments.

12. Quality of Infrastructure facilities: The quality viewed at three levels (i) Low Quality, (ii) Medium Quality and (iii) High Quality.

4

Analysis and Interpretation of Data - I

4.0. Introduction

The data collected through the opinionnaire from the 650 parents and community members has been analyzed and interpreted in Chapter IV and Chapter V. For the sake of clear analysis the variables identified are:

Independent Variables : (1) Age (2) Gender (3) Caste (4) Religion (5) Education (6) Income and (7) Occupation.

The dependent variables that are studied in these two chapters are :

(1) Availability of Infrastructural Facilities.

(2) Health Care.

(3) Curriculum Suitability.

(4) Monitoring.

(5) Quality of Infrastructural Facilities.

(6) Teacher Participation.

(7) Learning Environment.

The association between each one of the seven independent variables with each one of the seven dependent variables has been studied. Tabular representation together with their percentages are given. The Statistical analysis has been done with the help of x^2 test.

In this chapter the association between seven of the independent variables with the three of the dependent variables is under taken. The remaining four dependent variables and their association with the independent variables is undertaken in chapter V.

4.1.1. Age Background vs Opinions of the Respondents with respect to the availability of Infrastructure facilities in Balawadees

In order to study the influence of age background and the opinions of the respondents with respect to the availability of infrastructure facilities in Balawadees, seven items contained in the opinionnaire, under infrastructural facilities were included in the tool provided to the respondents. The responses of the parents / community members are analyzed and presented below:

Majority of the age groups, i.e., 21 to 50 old felt that the infrastructure facilities are of medium level. Whereas the older age group who are 51 years and above felt that the infrastructure facilities are of low level. On the whole majority of the respondents 49.7% opined that the infrastructure facilities are of medium level.

4.1.1b. The Chi-square Values of the Responses

Item	*Value*
Calculated Value	170.953
Standard table value	16.81
Degrees of freedom	6
Levels of significance	0.01

4.1.1a. Frequency Distribution and Percentages

AGE in years		*AVA.INFR*			*Total*
		Low	*Medium*	*High*	
21 to 30	Count	42	79	9	130
	% within AGE	32.3%	60.8%	6.9%	100.0%
	% of Total	6.5%	12.2%	1.4%	20.0%
31-40	Count	38	126	13	177
	% within AGE	21.5%	71.2%	7.3%	100.0%
	% of Total	5.8%	19.4%	2.0%	27.2%
41-50	Count	38	92	83	213
	% within AGE	17.8%	43.2%	39.0%	100.0%
	% of Total	5.8%	14.2%	12.8%	32.8%
51 and above	Count	82	26	22	130
	% within AGE	63.1%	20.0%	16.9%	100.0%
	% of Total	12.6%	4.0%	3.4%	20.0%
TOTAL	Count	200	323	127	650
	% within AGE	39.8%	49.7%	19.5%	100.0%
	% of Total	30.8%	49.7%	19.5%	100.00%

Since, the calculated chi-square value is more than the table value, the null hypothesis is rejected and it is concluded seen that there is an association between the age structure and their opinion on the availability of facilities.

4.1.2. The Gender Background vs Opinions of the Respondents with respect of the availability of Infrastructure facilities in Balawadees

In order to study the influence of gender on the opinions of the respondents with respect to the availability of infrastructure facilities in balawadees. The responses of the parents / community members are analyzed and presented below:

4.1.2a. Frequency Distribution and Percentages

Gender			*AVA.INFR*			*Total*
			Low	*Medium*	*High*	
Male	1.0	Count	118	172	35	325
		% within Gender	36.3%	52.9%	10.8%	100.0%
		% of Total	18.2%	26.5%	5.4%	50.0%
Female	2.0	Count	82	151	92	325
		% within Gender	25.2%	46.5%	28.3%	100.0%
		% of Total	12.6%	23.2%	14.2%	50.0%
TOTAL		Count	200	323	127	650
		% within Gender	30.8%	49.7%	19.5%	100.0%
		% of Total	30.8%	49.7%	19.5%	100.0%

Majority of Respondent felt that the availability of infrastructure is of medium level. However, 14.2% of the Females as against 5.4% Males felt that the facilities are high.

4.1.2 b. The Chi-square values of the responses

The null hypothesis has been tested by the chi-square non-parametric statistical technique and the results obtained are interpreted at 99% level of confidence.

Since, the calculated value is more than the table value, the null hypothesis is rejected and it is seen that "There is an association between Sex of Parents and Community Members and their opinions about the availability of infrastructure facilities in Balawadees".

4.1.2b. The Chi-square Values of Responses

Item	*Value*
Calculated Value	-33.428
Standard table value	9.21
Degrees of freedom	2
Levels of significance	0.01

4.1.3. The Caste Background vs Opinions of the Respondents with respect of the availability of Infrastructure facilities in Balawadees

4.1.3a. Frequency Distribution and Percentages

Caste		*AVA.INFR*			*Total*
		Low	*Medium*	*High*	
SC	Count	48	154	19	221
	% within caste	21.7%	69.7%	8.6%	100.0%
	% of Total	7.4%	23.7%	2.9%	34.0%
ST	Count	69	86	19	174
	% within caste	39.7%	49.4%	10.9%	100.0%
	% of Total	10.6%	13.2%	2.9%	26.8%
BC	Count	46	66	79	191
	% within caste	24.1%	34.6%	41.4%	100.0%
	% of Total	7.1%	10.2%	12.2%	29.4%
OC	Count	37	17	10	64
	% within caste	57.8%	26.6%	15.6%	100.0%
	% of Total	5.7%	2.6%	1.5%	9.8%
TOTAL	Count	200	323	127	650
	% within caste	30.8%	49.7%	19.5%	100.0%
	% of Total	30.8%	49.7%	19.5%	100.0%

In order to study the influence of caste background and the opinions of the respondents with respect to the availability of infrastructure facilities in balawadees, The responses of the parents / community members are analyzed and presented below:

While majority of SC's & ST's said that the availability of Infrastructural facilities in Balawadees is medium. The majority of BC's felt that availability of Infrastructural facilities in Balawadees is High. Whereas majority of the OC's felt that availability of Infrastructural facilities in Balawadees is low. This indicates that there is influence of caste on the opinion on availability of Infrastructural facilities in Balawadees.

4.1.3b. The Chi-square Values of the Responses

Item	*Value*
Calculated Value	129.00
Standard table value	16.81
Degrees of freedom	6
Levels of significance	0.01

Since, the calculated value is more than the table value, the null hypothesis is rejected, indicating that "There is an association between Caste background of the respondents and their opinions about the availability of infrastructure facilities in Balawadees".

4.1.4. The Religious Background vs Opinions of the Respondents with respect to the availability of Infrastructure facilities in Balawadees

In order to study the influence of Religious background and the opinions of the respondents with respect to the availability of infrastructure facilities in balawadees, the responses of the parents / community members are analyzed and presented below:

As seen from the above table majority of Muslims felt that felt that availability of Infrastructural facilities in Balawadees is low. Majority of Hindus said that availability of Infrastructural facilities

4.1.4a. Frequency Distribution and Percentages

Religion		*AVA.INFR*			*Total*
		Low	*Medium*	*High*	
Muslims	Count	161	56	43	260
	% within RELIGION	61.9%	21.5%	16.5%	100.0%
	% of Total	24.8%	8.6%	6.6%	40.0%
Hindus	Count		249	11	260
	% within religion		95.8%	4.2%	100.0%
	% of Total		38.3%	1.7%	40.0%
Christians	Count	28	14	70	112
	% within RELIGION	25.0%	12.5%	62.5%	100.0%
	% of Total	4.3%	2.2%	10.8%	17.2%
Others	Count	11	4	3	18
	% within RELIGION	61.1%	22.2%	16.7%	100%
	% of Total	1.7%	6%	5%	2.8%
TOTAL	Count	200	323	127	650
	% within RELIGION	30.8%	49.7%	19.5%	100.0%
	% of Total	30.8%	49.7%	19.5%	100.0%

in Balawadees is Medium. Majority of Christians have said that availability of Infrastructural facilities in Balawadees is High.

This variation indicates the influence of religion on opinion about availability of Infrastructural facilities in Balawadees. It further indicates that the Balawadees located in different community localities do have a significant variation in the availability of infrastructural facilities.

4.1.4b. The Chi-square Values of the Responses

Item	*Value*
Calculated Value	493.332
Standard table value	16.81
Degrees of freedom	6
Levels of significance	0.01

Since, the calculated value is more than the table value, the null hypothesis is rejected and it is seen that "There is an association between religious background of the respondents and their opinions about the availability of infrastructure facilities in balawadees".

4.1.5. Education Background vs Opinions of the Respondents with respect to the availability of Infrastructure facilities in Balawadees

In order to study the influence of Educational background and the opinions of the respondents with respect to the availability of infrastructure facilities in balawadees the responses of the parents / community members are analyzed and presented below:

The results indicate that the majority of respondents who are illiterates with those who have 11 to 15 years education together felt that the infrastructure facilities are of low. On the other hands the respondents with upto 5 years schooling opined that the infrastructure facilities are of medium whereas most of the respondents with 6 to 10 years education felt that the infrastructure facilities are of high level.

4.1.5a. Frequency Distribution and Percentages

Education		*AVA.INFR*			*Total*
		Low	*Medium*	*High*	
Non Literates	Count	153	116	45	314
	% within eduation	48.7%	36.9%	14.3%	100.0%
	% of Total	23.5%	17.8%	6.9%	48.3%
5 years of Schooling	Count	36	203	20	259
	% within Education	13.9%	78.4%	7.7%	100.0%
	% of Total	5.5%	31.2%	3.1%	39.8%
6 to 10 years of schooling	Count	2		61	63
	% within Education	3.2%		96.8%	100.0%
	% of Total	3%		9.4%	9.7%
11 to 15 years of Schooling	Count	9	4	1	14
	% within Education	64.3%	28.6%	7.1%	100.0%
	% of Total	1.4%	6%	2%	2.2%
TOTAL	Count	200	323	127	650
	% within Education	30.8%	49.7%	19.5%	100.0%
	% of Total	30.8%	49.7%	19.5%	100.0%

4.1.5b. The Chi-square Values of the Responses

Item	*Value*
Calculated Value	379.858
Standard table value	16.81
Degrees of freedom	6
Levels of significance	0.01

Since, the calculated value is more than the table value, the null hypothesis is rejected indicting "There is an association between Educational background of the respondents and their opinions about the availability of infrastructure facilities in balawadees".

4.1.6. Income Background vs Opinions of the Respondents with respect to the availability of Infrastructure facilities in Balawadees

In order to study the influence of Income background and the opinions of the respondents with respect to the availability of

4.1.6a. Frequency Distribution and Percentages

INCOME in Rupees per month		*AVA.INFR*			*Total*
		Low	*Medium*	*High*	
Upto Rs.1,500	Count	109	111	23	243
	% within income	44.9%	45.7%	9.5%	100.0%
	% of Total	16.8%	17.1%	3.5%	37.4%
Rs.1501 to 3000	Count	44	144	24	212
	% within Income	20.8%	67.9%	11.3%	100.0%
	% of Total	6.8%	22.2%	3.7%	32.6%
Rs.3001 and above	Count	47	68	80	195
	% within Income	24.1%	34.9%	41.0%	100.0%
	% of Total	7.2%	10.5%	12.3%	30.0%
TOTAL	Count	200	323	127	650
	% within income	30.8%	49.7%	19.5%	100.0%
	% of Total	30.8%	49.7%	19.5%	100.0%

infrastructure facilities in balawadees, the responses of the parents / community members are analyzed and presented below:

As seen from the above table majority of respondents with monthly income up to Rs 1500 and other majority from the monthly income group between Rs.1501 to Rs.3000 felt that availability of Infrastructural facilities in Balawadees is Medium. Majority respondents with monthly income of Rs. 3001 and above felt that the availability of infrastructural facilities is high.

4.1.6b. The Chi-square Values of the Responses

Item	*Value*
Calculated Value	115.013
Standard table value	13.28
Degrees of freedom	4
Levels of significance	0.01

Since, the calculated value is more than the table value, the null hypothesis is rejected and it is concluded that "There is an association between Income background of the respondents and their opinions about the availability of infrastructure facilities in balawadees centers".

4.1.7. Occupation Background vs Opinions of the Respondents with respect to the availability of Infrastructure facilities in Balawadees

In order to study the influence of Occupation background and the opinions of the respondents with respect to the availability of infrastructure facilities in balawadees, the responses of the parents / community members are analyzed and presented below:

As evident from the above table majority of the daily wage workers / laborers felt that availability of Infrastructural facilities in

4.1.7a. Frequency Distribution and Percentages

Occupation		*AVA.INFR*			*Total*
		Low	*Medium*	*High*	
Daily wage workers / labourers	Count	90	44	21	155
	% within Occupation	58.1%	28.4%	13.5%	100.0%
	% of Total	13.8%	6.8%	3.2%	23.8%
Traditional Professional	Count	38	152	22	212
	% within Occupation	17.9%	71.7%	10.4%	100.0%
	% of Total	5.8%	23.4%	3.4%	32.6%
Service Govt./Pvt.	Count	47	71	77	195
	% within Occupation	24.1%	36.4%	39.5%	100.0%
	% of Total	7.2%	10.9%	11.8%	30.0%
Business	Count	25	56	7	88
	% within Occupation	28.4%	63.6%	8.0%	100.0%
	% of Total	3.8%	8.6%	1.1%	13.5%
TOTAL	Count	200	323	127	650
	% within Occupation	30.8%	49.7%	19.5%	100.0%
	% of Total	30.8%	49.7%	19.5%	100.0%

Balawadees is low. Majority of the service respondents in (Govt, and Pvt) felt that availability of Infrastructural facilities in Balawadees is high. Majority of Traditional and Professionals and Business group of respondents felt that available of Infrastructural facilities in Balawadees is medium level.

Since, the calculated value is more than the table value, the null hypothesis is rejected indicating that "There is an association between Occupational background of the respondents and their opinions about the availability of infrastructure facilities.

4.1.7b. The Chi-square Values of the Responses

Item	*Value*
Calculated Value	154.772
Standard table value	16.81
Degrees of freedom	6
Levels of significance	0.01%

4.2.1. Age Background vs Opinions of the Respondents with respect to the availability of Health Care facilities in Balawadees

In order to study the influence of age background on the opinions of the respondents with respect to the availability of health care facilities in balawadees, eleven items contained in the tool were examined. The responses of parents / community members are analyzed and presented below:

As seen from the above table majority of respondents from the age group of 21-30 years felt that Health care facilities are low. Majority from age group 31to 40 and 51 & above said that Health care facilities are medium. Majority of the respondents from 41 to 50 years felt that High.

4.2.1a. Frequency Distribution and Percentages

AGE in years		*HEAL.CAR*			*Total*
		Low	*Medium*	*High*	
21-30	Count	99	23	8	130
	% within Age	76.2%	17.7%	6.2%	100.0%
	% of Total	15.2%	3.5%	1.2%	20.0%
31-40	Count	59	94	24	177
	% within Age	33.3%	53.1%	13.6%	100.0%
	% of Total	9.1%	14.5%	3.7%	27.2%
41-50	Count	67	72	74	213
	% within Age	31.5%	33.8%	34.7%	100.0%
	% of Total	10.3%	11.1%	11.4%	32.8%
51 and above	Count	59	62	9	130
	% within Age	45.4%	47.7%	6.9%	100.0%
	% of Total	9.1%	9.5%	1.4%	20.0%
TOTAL	Count	284	251	115	650
	% within Age	43.7%	38.6%	17.7%	100.0%
	% of Total	43.7%	38.6%	17.7%	100.0%

4.2.1b. The Chi-square Values of the Responses

Item	*Value*
Calculated Value	126.510
Standard table value	16.81
Degrees of freedom	6
Levels of significance	0.01

Since, the calculated value is more than the table value, the null hypothesis is rejected and it is concluded that "There is an association between the Age background of the respondents and their opinions about the availability of health care facilities adopted in balawadees".

4.2.2. The Gender Background vs Opinions of the Respondents with respect to the availability of Health Care facilities in Balawadees

In order to study the influence of the Gender background on the opinions of the respondents with respect to the availability of health care facilities in balawadees, the responses of parents / community members are analyzed and presented below:

4.2.2a. Frequency Distribution and Percentages

Gender		*Heal.Car*			*Total*
		Low	*Medium*	*High*	
Male	Count % within Gender % of Total	207 63.7% 31.8%	89 27.4% 13.7%	29 8.9% 4.5%	325 100.0% 50.0%
Female	Count % within Gender % of Total	77 23.7% 11.8%	162 49.8% 24.9%	86 26.5% 13.2%	325 100.0% 50.0%
TOTAL	Count % within Gender % of Total	284 43.7% 43.7%	251 38.6% 38.6%	115 17.7% 17.7%	650 100.0% 100.0%

As evident from the above table Majority of Male respondents felt that Health care facilities are low. Where as Majority of Female respondents felt that availability of Health care facilities in Balawadees is Medium.

4.2.2b. The Chi-square Values of the Responses

Item	*Value*
Calculated Value	108.990
Standard table value	9.21
Degrees of freedom	2
Levels of significance	0.01

Since, the calculated value is more than the table value, the null hypothesis is rejected and it is concluded "There is an association between opinions of parents and community members gender background and their opinions about the availability of health care facilities adopted in balawadees".

4.2.3. The Caste vs Opinions of the Respondents with respect to availability of Health Care facilities in Balawadees

In order to study the influence of Caste background on the opinions of the respondents with respect to the availability of health care facilities in balawadees, the responses of parents / community members are analyzed and presented below:

4.2.3a. Frequency Distribution and Percentages

CASTE		*HEAL. CAR*			*Total*
		Low	*Medium*	*High*	
SC	Count	154	45	22	221
	% within Caste	69.7%	20.4%	10.0%	100.0%
	% of Total	23.7%	6.9%	3.4%	34.0%
ST	Count	22	137	15	174
	% within Caste	12.6%	78.7%	8.6%	100.0%
	% of Total	3.4%	21.1%	2.3%	26.8%
BC	Count	58	57	76	191
	% within Caste	30.4%	29.8%	39.8%	100.0%
	% of Total	8.9%	8.8%	11.7%	29.4%
OC	Count	50	12	2	64
	% within Caste	78.1%	18.8%	3.1%	100.0%
	% of Total	7.7%	1.8%	3%	9.8%
TOTAL	Count	284	251	115	650
	% within caste	43.7%	38.6%	17.7%	100.0%
	% of Total	43.7%	38.6%	17.7%	100.0%

As shown in the above table Majority of SC's and OC's said that Health Care facilities are low. Majority of ST's said that availability of Health care facilities in Balawadees is Medium. Majority of B.C's said that the availability of Health care facilities in Balawadees is High.

4.2.3b. The Chi-square Values of the Responses

Item	*Value*
Calculated Value	275.602
Standard table value	16.81
Degrees of freedom	6
Levels of significance	0.01

The above null hypothesis has been tested by chi-square non-parametric statistical technique and the results obtained are interpreted at 99% level of confidence.

Since, the calculated value is more than the table value, the null hypothesis is rejected it is concluded that "There is an association between the Caste background of the respondents and their opinions about the availability of health care facilities adopted in balawadees".

4.2.4. The Religious Background vs Opinions of the Respondents with respect to the availability of Health Care facilities in Balawadees

In order to study the influence of the Religious background on the opinions of the respondents with respect to the availability of health care facilities in balawadees, the responses of parents / community members are analyzed and presented below:

As seen from the above table Majority of Muslims felt that health care facility in Balawadees is Medium. Majority of Hindus said that the Health care facility facilities in Balawadees is Low. Majority of Christian said that available of Infrastructural facilities in Balawadees is High. 100% of respondents from the group of other religion said that Health care facilities are low. The cumulative Majority felt it as low level.

4.2.4a. Frequency Distribution and Percentages

RELIGION			*HEAL.CAR*			*Total*
			Low	*Medium*	*High*	
Muslims	1.0	Count	77	158	25	260
		% within Religion	29.6%	60.8%	9.6%	100.0%
		% of Total	11.8%	24.3%	3.8%	40.0%
Hindus	2.0	Count	156	79	25	260
		% within Religion	60.0%	30.4%	9.6%	100.0%
		% of Total	24.0%	12.2%	3.8%	40.0%
Christians	3.0	Count	33	14	65	112
		% within Religion	29.5%	12.5%	58.0%	100.0%
		% of Total	5.1%	2.2%	10.0%	2.8%
Others	4.0	Count	18			18
		% within Religion	100.0%			100.0%
		% of Total	2.8%			2.8%
TOTAL		Count	284	251	115	650
		% within Religion	43.7%	38.6%	17.7%	100.0%
		% of Total	43.7%	38.6%	17.7%	100.0%

4.2.4b. The Chi-square Values of the Responses

Item	*Value*
Calculated Value	235.599
Standard table value	16.81
Degrees of freedom	6
Levels of significance	0.01

The above null hypothesis has been tested by chi-square non-parametric statistical technique and the results obtained are interpreted at 99% level of confidence.

Since, the calculated value is more than the table value, the null hypothesis is rejected it concluded that "There is an association between the religious background of the respondents and their opinions about the availability of health care facilities adopted in balawadees".

4.2.5. Education Background vs Opinions of the Respondents with respect to the availability of Health Care facilities in Balawadees

In order to study the influence of the Educational background on the opinions of the respondents with respect to the availability of health care facilities in balawadees, the responses of parents / community members are analyzed and presented below:

As seen from the above table Majority of the illiterates opined that the health care facilities are low. Majority of the respondents with 5 years schooling along with 11 to 15 years of schooling opined the health care facilities are medium. Whereas Majority of the respondents with 6 to 10 years schooling said that the health care facilities are high.

Since, the calculated value is more than the table value, the null hypothesis is rejected it is concluded that "There is an association between the Educational background of the respondents and their opinions about the availability of health care facilities adopted in balawadees".

4.2.5a. Frequency Distribution and Percentages

Education		*Heal.Car*			*Total*
		Low	*Medium*	*High*	
Non Literates	Count	164	120	30	314
	% within Education	52.2%	38.2%	9.6%	100.0%
	% of Total	25.2%	18.5%	4.6%	48.3%
5 years of Schooling	Count	116	120	23	259
	% within Education	44.8%	46.3%	8.9%	100.0%
	% of Total	17.8%	18.5%	3.5%	39.8%
6 to 10 years of Schooling	Count	1	1	61	63
	% within Education	1.6%	1.6%	96.8%	100.0%
	% of Total	2%	2%	9.4%	9.7%
11 to 15 years of Schooling	Count	3	10	1	14
	% within Education	21.4%	71.4%	7.1%	100.0%
	% of Total	5%	1.5%	2%	2.2%
TOTAL	Count	284	251	115	650
	% within Education	43.7%	38.6%	17.7%	100.0%
	% of Total	43.7%	38.6%	17.7%	100.0%

4.2.5b. The Chi-square Values of the Responses

Item	*Value*
Calculated Value	309.724
Standard table value	16.81
Degrees of freedom	6
Levels of significance	0.01

4.2.6. Income Background vs Opinions of the Respondents with respect to the availability of Health Care facilities in Balawadees

In order to study the influence of the Income background on the opinions of the respondents with respect to the availability of health care facilities in balawadees, eleven items were constructed and provided to the respondents. The responses of parents / community members are analyzed and presented below:

4.2.6a. Frequency Distribution and Percentages

INCOME in Rupees per month		*HEAL.CAR*			*Total*
		Low	*Medium*	*High*	
Upto Rs.1500	Count % within Income % of Total	144 59.3% 22.2%	83 34.2% 12.8%	16 6.6% 2.5%	243 100.0% 37.4%
Rs.1501 to 3000	Count % within Income % of Total	80 37.7% 12.3%	111 52.4% 17.1%	21 9.9% 3.2%	212 100.0% 32.6%
Rs.3000 and above	Count % within Income % of Total	60 30.8% 9.2%	57 29.2% 8.8%	78 40.0% 12.0%	195 100.0% 30.0%
TOTAL	Count % within Income % of Total	284 43.7% 43.7%	251 38.6% 38.6%	115 17.7% 17.7%	650 100.0% 100.0%

4.2.6b. The Chi-square Values of the Responses

Item	*Value*
Calculated Value	117.780
Standard table value	13.28
Degrees of freedom	4
Levels of significance	0.01

As seen from the above table Majority of respondents from the monthly income of rupees 1500 felt that health care facilities in Balawadees is low. Majority from income group of Rs 1501 to 3000 said that the Health care facilities in Balawadees is Medium. Majority of respondent from income group 3001 and above said that Health care facilities in Balawadees is High.

The null hypothesis has been tested by chi-square non-parametric statistical technique and the results obtained are interpreted at 99% level of confidence.

Since, the calculated value is more than the table value, the null hypothesis is rejected and it is concluded that "There is an association between the income background of the respondents and their opinions about the availability of health care facilities adopted in balawadees".

4.2.7. The Occupation Background vs Opinions of the Respondents with respect to the availability of Health Care facilities in Balawadees

In order to study the influence of the Occupation background on the opinions of the respondents with respect to the availability of health care facilities in balawadees, eleven items were constructed and provided to the respondents. The responses of parents / community members are analyzed and presented below:

As seen from the above table Majority of Daily wage workers / labourers felt with business group felt that health care facilities in Balawadees is Low. Majority of Traditional and Professional groups

4.2.7a. Frequency Distribution and Percentages

Occupation		*Heal.Car*			*Total*
		Low	*Medium*	*High*	
Daily Wage workers / labourers	Count	83	59	13	155
	% within Occupation	53.5%	38.1%	8.4%	100.0%
	% of Total	12.8%	9.1%	2.0%	23.8%
Traditional Professional	Count	84	112	16	212
	% within Occupation	39.6%	52.8%	7.5%	100.0%
	% of Total	12.9%	17.2%	2.5%	32.6%
Service Govt./Pvt.	Count	59	60	76	195
	% within Occupation	30.3%	30.8%	39.0%	100.0%
	% of Total	9.1%	9.2%	11.7%	30.0%
Business	Count	58	20	10	88
	% within Occupation	65.9%	22.7%	11.4%	100.0%
	% of Total	8.9%	3.1%	1.5%	13.5%
TOTAL	Count	284	251	115	650
	% within Occupation	43.7%	38.6%	17.7%	100.0%
	% of Total	43.7%	38.6%	17.7%	100.0%

felt that Health care in Balawadees is Medium. Majority of Govt, Service respondents felt that of Health care in Balawadees is High.

4.2.7b. The Chi-square Values of the Responses

Item	*Value*
Calculated Value	114.046
Standard table value	16.81
Degrees of freedom	6
Levels of significance	0.01

The null hypothesis has been tested by chi-square non-parametric statistical technique and the results obtained are interpreted at 99% level of confidence.

Since, the calculated value is more than the table value, the null hypothesis is rejected and it is concluded that "There is an association between the Occupation background of the respondents and their opinions about the availability of health care facilities adopted in balawadees".

4.3.1. Age Background vs Opinions of the Respondents with Respect to the Curriculum Suitability Adopted in Balawadees

In order to study the influence of age background on the opinions of the respondents with respect to the curriculum suitability adopted in balawadees, eight items were constructed and provided to the respondents. The responses of parents / community members are analyzed and presented below:

As seen from the above table Majority of respondents from age group of 21-30 years felt that curriculum suitability is low. Majority from age group 31-40 years felt that curriculum suitability is Medium. Majority from age group 41 to 50 years with 50 years and above group of respondents felt that curriculum suitability is low.

The null hypothesis has been tested by chi-square non-parametric statistical technique and the results obtained are interpreted at 99% level of confidence..

4.3.1a. Frequency Distribution and Percentages

AGE in years		*CURRI.SU*			*Total*
		Low	*Medium*	*High*	
21-30	Count	90	22	18	130
	% within Age	69.2%	16.9%	13.8%	100.0%
	% of Total	13.8%	3.4%	2.8%	20.0%
31-40	Count	40	95	42	177
	% within Age	22.6%	53.7%	23.7%	100.00%
	% of Total	6.2%	14.6%	6.5%	27.2%
41-50	Count	96	66	51	213
	% within Age	45.1%	31.0%	23.9%	100.0%
	% of Total	14.8%	10.2%	7.8%	32.8%
51 and above	Count	85	26	19	130
	% within Age	65.4%	20.0%	14.6%	100.0%
	% of Tota	13.1%	4.0%	2.9%	20.0%
TOTAL	Count	311	209	130	650
	% within Age	47.8%	32.2%	20.0%	100.0%
	% of Total	47.8%	32.2%	20.0%	100.0%

4.3.1b. The Chi-square Values of the Responses

Item	*Value*
Calculated Value	92.870
Standard table value	16.81
Degrees of freedom	6
Levels of significance	0.01

Since, the calculated value is more than the table value, the null hypothesis is rejected and it is concluded that "There is an association between the Age background of the respondents and their opinions about the curriculum suitability adopted in balawadees".

4.3.2. The Gender Background vs Opinions of the Respondents with Respect to the Curriculum Suitability Adopted in Balawadees

In order to study the influence of Gender background on the opinions of the respondents with respect to the curriculum suitability adopted in balawadees, the responses of parents / community members are analyzed and presented below:

4.3.2a. Frequency Distribution and Percentages

Gender		*Curri.SU*			*Total*
		Low	*Medium*	*High*	
Male	Count % within Gender % of Total	127 39.1% 19.5%	130 40.0% 20.0%	68 20.9% 10.5%	325 100.0% 50.0%
Female	Count % within Gender % of Total	184 56.6% 28.3%	79 24.3% 12.2%	62 19.1% 9.5%	325 100.0% 50.0%
TOTAL	Count % within Gender % of Total	311 47.8% 47.8%	209 32.2% 32.2%	130 20.0% 20.0%	650 100.0% 100.0%

As seen from the above table Majority of male respondents expressed that curriculum suitability is Medium Level. Majority of female respondents felt that curriculum suitability is low indicating gender influence.

4.3.2b. The Chi-square Values of the Responses

Item	*Value*
Calculated Value	23.169
Standard table value	9.21
Degrees of freedom	2
Levels of significance	0.01

Since, the calculated value is more than the table value, the null hypothesis is rejected and it is concluded that "There an association between the gender background of the respondents and their opinions about the curriculum suitability adopted in balawadees".

4.3.3. The Caste Background vs Opinions of the Respondents with Respect to the Curriculum Suitability Adopted in Balawadees

In order to study the influence of caste background on the opinions of the respondents with respect to the curriculum suitability adopted in balawadees, the responses of parents / community members are analyzed and presented below:

Irrespective of caste all respondents opined that the curriculum suitability is low.

The null hypothesis has been tested by chi-square non-parametric statistical technique and the results obtained are interpreted at 95% level of confidence.

Since, the calculated value is more than the table value, the null hypothesis is rejected and it is concluded that "There is an association between the Caste background of the respondents and their opinions about the curriculum suitability adopted in balawadees".

4.3.3a. Frequency Distribution and Percentages

Caste		*Curri.SU*			*Total*
		Low	*Medium*	*High*	
SC	Count	101	83	37	221
	% within Caste	45.7%	16.7%	16.7%	100.0%
	% of Total	15.5%	5.7%	5.7%	34.0%
ST	Count	75	54	45	174
	% within Caste	43.1%	31.0%	25.9%	100.0%
	% of Total	11.5%	8.3%	6.9%	26.8%
BC	Count	94	59	38	191
	% within caste	49.2%	30.9%	19.9%	100.0%
	% of Total	14.5%	9.1%	5.8%	29.4%
OC	Count	41	13	10	64
	% within Caste	64.1%	20.3%	15.6%	100.0%
	% of Total	6.3%	2.0%	1.5%	9.8%
TOTAL	Count	311	209	130	650
	% within Caste	47.8%	32.2%	20.0%	100.0%
	% of Total	47.8%	32.2%	20.0%	100.0%

4.3.3b. The Chi-square Values of the Responses

Item	*Value*
Calculated Value	14.359
Standard table value	12.59
Degrees of freedom	6
Levels of significance	0.05

4.3.4. The Religious Background vs Opinions of the Respondents with Respect to the Curriculum Suitability Adopted in Balawadees

In order to study the influence of Religious background on the opinions of the respondents with respect to the curriculum suitability adopted in balawadees, the responses of parents / community members are analyzed and presented below:

4.3.4a. Frequency Distribution and Percentages

Religion		*Curri.SU*			*Total*
		Low	*Medium*	*High*	
Muslims	Count	170	47	43	260
	% within Religion	65.4%	18.1%	16.5%	100.0%
	% of Total	26.2%	7.2%	6.6%	40.0%
Hindus	Count	46	147	67	260
	% within Religion	17.7%	56.5%	25.8%	100.0%
	% of Total	7.1%	22.6%	10.3%	40.0%
Christians	Count	91	9	12	112
	% within Religion	81.3%	8.0%	10.7%	100.0%
	% of Total	14.0%	1.4%	1.8%	17.2%
Others	Count	4	6	8	18
	% within Religion	22.2%	33.3%	44.4%	100.0%
	% of Total	6%	9%	1.2%	2.8%
TOTAL	Count	311	209	130	650
	% within Religion	47.8%	32.2%	20.0%	100.0%
	% of Total	47.8%	32.2%	20.0%	100.0%

As seen from the above table Majority of Muslims along with the Christians felt curriculum suitability is Low. Majority of Hindus said that curriculum suitability is Middle Level. The variation in the opinions indicates the influence of the religions over the curriculum suitability. There is need to review the curriculum followed in Balawadees.

4.3.4b. The Chi-square Values of the Responses

Item	*Value*
Calculated Value	195.179
Standard table value	16.81
Degrees of freedom	6
Levels of significance	0.01

Since, the calculated value is more than the table value, the null hypothesis is rejected. In other words, the alternative hypothesis has been accepted i.e., "There is a association between the Age background of the respondents and their opinions about the curriculum suitability adopted in balawadees".

4.3.5. Education Background vs Opinions of the Respondents with Respect to the Curriculum Suitability Adopted in Balawadees

In order to study the influence of Educational background on the opinions of the respondents with respect to the curriculum suitability adopted in balawadees, the responses of parents / community members are analyzed and presented below:

As seen in the above table Majority of non literate of 6 to 10 years schooling along with respondents 11 to 15 years of felt that curriculum suitability is low. Majority of 5 years schooling however felt that it is Medium.

Since, the calculated value is more than the table value, the null hypothesis is rejected it is concluded that "There is an association between the Educational background of the respondents and their opinions about the curriculum suitability adopted in balawadees".

4.3.5a. Frequency Distribution and Percentages

Education		*Curri.SU*			*Total*
		Low	*Medium*	*High*	
Non Literates	Count	159	92	63	314
	% within Education	50.6%	29.3%	20.1%	100.0%
	% of Total	24.5%	14.2%	9.7%	48.3%
5 years of Schooling	Count	89	113	57	259
	% within Education	34.4%	43.6%	22.0%	100.0%
	% of Total	13.7%	17.4%	8.8%	39.8%
6 to 10 years of Schooling	Count	51	2	10	63
	% within Education	81.0%	3.2%	15.9%	100.0%
	% of Total	7.8%	3%	1.5%	9.7%
11 to 15 years of Schooling	Count	12	2		14
	% within Education	85.7%	14.3%		100.0%
	% of Total	1.8%	3%		2.2%
TOTAL	Count	311	209	130	650
	% within Education	47.8%	32.2%	20.0%	100.0%
	% of Total	47.8%	32.2%	20.0%	100.0%

4.3.5b. The Chi-square Values of the Responses

Item	*Value*
Calculated Value	62.086
Standard table value	16.81
Degrees of freedom	6
Levels of significance	0.01

4.3.6. The Income Background vs Opinions of the Respondents with Respect to the Curriculum Suitability Adopted in Balawadees

In order to study the influence of Income background on the opinions of the respondents with respect to the curriculum suitability adopted in balawadees, the responses of parents / community members are analyzed and presented below:

4.3.6a. Frequency Distribution and Percentages

INCOME in Rupees per month		*CURRI.SU*			*Total*
		Low	*Medium*	*High*	
Upto Rs.1500	Count	162	41	40	243
	% within Income	66.7%	16.9%	16.5%	100.0%
	% of Total	24.9%	6.3%	6.2%	37.4%
Rs.1501 to 3000	Count	53	107	52	212
	% within Income	25.0%	50.5%	24.5%	100.0%
	% of Total	8.2%	16.5%	8.0%	32.6%
Rs. 3001 and above	Count	96	61	38	195
	% within Income	49.2%	31.3%	19.5%	100.0%
	% of Total	14.8%	9.4%	5.8%	30.0%
TOTAL	Count	311	209	130	650
	% within Income	47.8%	32.2%	20.0%	100.0%
	% of Total	47.8%	32.2%	20.0%	100.0%

As seen in the above table majority of respondents with up to Rs.1500 income and high income groups together felt that curriculum suitability is Low. Half of respondents with income range of Rs.1501 to Rs.3000 felt that curriculum suitability is medium.

4.3.6b. The Chi-square Values of the Responses

Item	*Value*
Calculated Value	84.733
Standard table value	13.28
Degrees of freedom	4
Levels of significance	0.01

Since, the calculated value is more than the table value, the null hypothesis is rejected and it is concluded that "There is an association between the Income background of the respondents and their opinions about the curriculum suitability adopted in balawadees".

4.3.7. The Occupation Background vs Opinions of the Respondents with Respect to the Curriculum Suitability Adopted in Balawadees

In order to study the influence of Occupation background on the opinions of the respondents with respect to the curriculum suitability adopted in balawadees, the responses of parents / community members are analyzed and presented below:

As seen in the above table majority of respondents from the daily wage / Labours along with Traditional and Professional group and service Govt. Pvt. said that curriculum suitability is Low. Majority of respondents from Business category felt that the curriculum suitability is Medium.

Since, the calculated value is more than the table value, the null hypothesis is rejected and it is concluded that "There is an association between the Occupation background of the respondents and their opinions about the curriculum suitability adopted in balawadees".

4.3.7a. Frequency Distribution and Percentages

Occupation		Curri.SU			Total
		Low	Medium	High	
Daily wages workers / labourers	Count	87	31	37	155
	% within Occupation	56.1%	20.0%	23.9%	100.0%
	% of Total	13.4%	4.8%	5.7%	23.8%
Traditional Professional	Count	88	73	51	212
	% within Occupation	41.5%	34.4%	24.1%	100.0%
	% of Total	13.5%	11.2%	7.8%	32.6%
Service Govt./Pvt.	Count	96	63	36	195
	% within Occupation	49.2%	32.3%	18.5%	100.0%
	% of Total	14.8%	9.7%	5.5%	30.0%
Business	Count	40	42	6	88
	% within Occupation	45.5%	47.7%	6.8%	100.0%
	% of Total	6.2%	6.5%	9%	13.5%
TOTAL	Count	311	209	130	650
	% within Occupation	47.8%	32.2%	20.0%	100.0%
	% of Total	47.8%	32.2%	20.0%	100.0%

4.3.7b. The Chi-square Values of the Responses

Item	*Value*
Calculated Value	29.070
Standard table value	16.81
Degrees of freedom	6
Levels of significance	0.01

5

Analysis and Interpretation of Data – II

OPINIONS OF PARENTS AND COMMUNITY MEMBERS (RESPONDENTS) ON THE WORKING OF BALWADIES IN TWIN CITIES

5.0. Introduction

In continuation with the previous chapter the association between each one of the seven independent variables with each one of dependent variables namely the monitoring on Balawadees centers, quality of infrastructure, Teacher participation and learning environment of Balawadee Centers has been taken up for study. After tabular representation together with their percentage are given. The statistical analysis with the help of the c^2 test is done.

In this chapter the data collected has been processed and analysed with respect to the following independent variables.

1. Age Level
2. Gender
3. Caste
4. Religion
5. Education
6. Income
7. Occupation

5.1.1. Age Background Vs Opinions of the Respondents with Respect to the Monitoring in Balawadees

In order to study the influence of age background on the opinions of the respondents with respect to the monitoring of balawadees, six items were constructed and provided to the respondents. The responses of the parents/ community members are analyzed and presented below :

5.1.1a. Frequency Distribution and Percentages

AGE in years		*MONITORING*			*Total*
		Low	*Medium*	*High*	
21-30	Count	102	16	12	130
	% within AGE	78.5%	12.3%	9.2%	100.0%
	% of Total	15.7%	2.5%	1.8%	20.0%
31-40	Count	63	110	4	177
	% within AGE	35.6%	62.1%	2.3%	100.0%
	% of Total	9.7%	16.9%	6%	27.2%
41-50	Count	75	76	62	213
	% within AGE	35.2%	35.7%	29.1%	100.0%
	% of Total	11.5%	11.7%	9.5%	32.8%
51 and above	Count	101	22	7	130
	% within AGE	77.7%	16.9%	5.4%	100.0%
	% of Total	15.5%	3.4%	1.1%	20.0%
TOTAL	Count	341	224	85	650
	% within AGE	52.5%	34.5%	13.1%	100.0%
	% of Total	52.5%	34.5%	13.1%	100.0%

As seen in the above table majority of respondents from the age group of 21-30 and 51 and above have given the opinion that the of monitoring in Balawadees is Low. Majority of respondents from age group 31 to 40 and 41 to 50 years said that the monitoring is medium.

The null hypothesis has been tested by chi-square non-parametric statistical technique and the results obtained are interpreted at 99% level of confidence.

5.1.2b. The Chi-square Values of the Responses

Item	*Value*
Calculated Value	58.140
Standard table value	9.21
Degrees of freedom	2
Levels of Significance	0.01

As the calculated value is more than the table value, the null hypothesis is rejected and it is concluded that "There is an association between the Age background of the respondents and their opinions about the monitoring on balawadees.

5.1.2. The Gender Background Vs Opinions of the Respondents with Respect to the Monitoring of Balawadees

In order to study the influence of the Gender background on the opinions of the respondents with respect to the monitoring of balawadees, six items were constructed and provided to the respondents. The responses of the parents/community members are analyzed and presented below :

5.1.2a. Frequency Distribution and Percentages

GENDER		*MONITORING*			*Total*
		Low	*Medium*	*High*	
Male	Count	169	143	13	325
	% within GENDER	52.0%	44.0%	4.0%	100.0%
	% of Total	26.0%	22.0%	2.0%	50.0%
Female	Count	172	81	72	325
	% within GENDER	52.9%	24.9%	22.2%	100.0%
	% of Total	26.5%	12.5%	11.1%	50.0%
TOTAL	Count	341	224	85	650
	% within GENDER	52.5%	34.5%	13.1%	100.0%
	% of Total	52.5%	34.5%	13.1%	100.0%

As seen from the above table majority of female and male respondents in felt that the monitoring in Balawadees is low. The responses from both male and female respondents firmly indicates that the monitoring in Balawadees is low.

5.1.2b. The Chi-square Values of the Responses

Item	*Value*
Calculated Value	58.140
Standard table value	9.21
Degrees of freedom	2
Levels of Significance	0.01

As the calculated value is more than the table value, the null hypothesis is rejected and it is concluded that "There an association between the Gender background of the respondents and their opinions about the monitoring of balawadees.

5.1.3. The Caste Background Vs Opinions of the Respondents with Respect to the Monitoring of Balawadees

In order to study the influence of the caste background on the opinions of the respondents with respect to the Teacher performance in balawadees, six items were constructed and provided to the respondents. The responses of the parents / community members are analyzed and presented below :

As seen from the above table Majority from all four cast groups felt that monitoring in balawadees is low, indicating need to improve monitoring on balawadees.

As the calculated value is more than the table value, the null hypothesis is rejected and it is concluded that "There is an association between the caste background of the respondents and their opinions about the Monitoring in balawadees.

5.1.3a. Frequency Distribution and Percentages

CASTE		*MONITORING*			*Total*
		Low	*Medium*	*High*	
SC	Count	120	84	17	221
	% within CASTE	54.3%	38.0%	7.7%	100.0%
	% of Total	18.5%	12.9%	2.6%	34.0%
ST	Count	105	61	8	174
	% within CASTE	60.3%	35.1%	4.6%	100.0%
	% of Total	16.2%	9.4%	1.2%	26.8%
BC	Count	67	65	59	191
	% within CASTE	35.1%	34.0%	30.9%	100.0%
	% of Total	10.3%	10.0%	9.1%	29.4%
Others	Count	49	14	1	64
	% within CASTE	76.6%	21.9%	1.6%	100.0%
	% of Total	7.5%	2.2%	2%	9.8%
TOTAL	Count	341	224	85	650
	% within CASTE	52.5%	34.5%	13.1%	100.0%
	% of Total	52.5%	34.5%	13.1%	100.0%

5.1.3b. The Chi-Square Values of the Responses

Item	*Value*
Calculated Value	91.369
Standard table value	16.81
Degrees of freedom	6
Levels of Significance	0.01

5.1.4. The Religious Background Vs Opinions to the Respondents with Respect to the Monitoring of Balawadees

In order to study the influence of the Religous background on the opinions of the respondents with respect to the monitoring of balawadees, six items were constructed and provided to the respondents. The responses of the parents/community members are analyzed and presented below :

5.1.4a. Frequency Distribution and Percentages

RELIGION		*MONITORING*			*Total*
		Low	*Medium*	*High*	
Muslims	Count	205	35	20	260
	% within RELIGION	78.8%	13.5%	7.7%	100.0%
	% of Total	31.5%	5.4%	3.1%	40.0%
Hindus	Count	79	170	11	260
	% within RELIGION	30.4%	65.4%	4.2%	100.0%
	% of Total	12.2%	26.2%	1.7%	40.0%
Christians	Count	44	14	54	112
	% within RELIGION	39.3%	12.5%	48.2%	100.0%
	% of Total	6.8%	2.2%	8.3%	17.2%
Others	Count	13	5		18
	% within RELIGION	72.2%	27.8%		100.0%
	% of Total	2.0%	8%		2.8%
TOTAL	Count	341	224	85	650
	% within RELIGION	52.5%	34.5%	13.1%	100.0%
	% of Total	52.5%	34.5%	13.1%	100.0%

As seen from the above table majority from Muslims and other castes, opined that the monitoring of Balawadees is low. Hindus in majority said that Monitoring is Medium. While majority of Christian have said that monitoring is High. 72.2% of respondents from other religions said that Monitoring facilities in Balawadees is Low.

5.1.4b. The Chi-square Values to the Responses

Item	*Value*
Calculated Value	314.447
Standard table value	16.81
Degrees of freedom	6
Levels of Significance	0.01

Since the calculated value is more than the table value, the null hypothesis is rejected and is concluded that. "There is an association between the religious background of the respondents and their opinions about the Monitoring adopted in balawadees.

5.1.5. The Educational Background Vs Opinions of the Respondents with respect to the Monitoring of Balawadees

In order to study the influence of the Educational background on the opinions of the respondents with respect to the monitoring of balawadees, six items were constructed and provided to the respondents. The responses of the parents/community members are analyzed and presented below :

As seen from above table majority of non-literates and equal no. of 11 to 15 years schooling category of respondents said that monitoring on Balawadees low. Majority of respondents with 5 years schooling said that the monitoring facilities in Balawadees in Medium. Majority from 6 to 10 years of schooling said that monitoring in Balawadees is High. It is interesting to note that majority from 11 to 15 yrs schooling and non-literates gave the

5.1.5a. Frequency Distribution and Percentages

EDUCATION		*MONITORING*			*Total*
		Low	*Medium*	*High*	
Non Literates	Count	202	93	19	314
	% within EDUCATION	64.3%	29.6%	6.1%	100.0%
	% of Total	31.1%	14.3%	2.9%	48.3%
5 years of Schooling	Count	120	124	15	259
	% within EDUCATION	46.3%	47.9%	5.8%	100.0%
	% of Total	18.5%	19.1%	2.3%	39.8%
6 to 10 years of Schooling	Count	7	5	51	63
	% within EDUCATION	11.1%	7.9%	81.0%	100.0%
	% of Total	1.1%	8%	7.85	9.7%
10 to 15 years of Schooling	Count	12	2		14
	% within EDUCATION	85.7%	14.3%		100.0%
	% of Total	1.8%	3%		2.2%
TOTAL	Count	341	224	85	650
	% within EDUCATION	52.5%	34.5%	13.1%	100.0%
	% of Total	52.5%	34.5%	13.1%	100.0%

same opinion that monitoring is Low, indicating need to review monitoring.

5.1.5b. The Chi-square Values of the Responses

Item	*Value*
Calculated Value	310.100
Standard table value	16.81
Degrees of freedom	6
Levels of Significance	0.01

As the calculated value is more than the table value, the null hypothesis is rejected and it is concluded that. "There an association between the Educational background of the respondents and their opinions about the monitoring of balawadees".

5.1.6. The Income Background Vs Opinions of the Respondents With Respect to the Monitoring of Balawadees

In order to study the influence of income background on the opinions of the respondents with respect to the monitoring of balawadees, six items were constructed and provided to the respondents. The responses of the parents/community members are analyzed and presented below :

As seen from the above table majority of respondents with monthly income upto Rs 1500 and the high income groups said that the Monitoring facilities in Balawadees Low. The majority from monthly income between Rs. 1500 to 3000 felt that monitoring in Balawadees is Medium.

Since the calculated value is more than the table value, the null hypothesis is rejected indicating that "There an association between the income background of the respondents and their opinions about the monitoring adopted in balawadees.

5.1.6a. Frequency Distribution and Percentages

INCOME in Rupees per month		*MONITORING*			*Total*
		Low	*Medium*	*High*	
Upto 1500	Count	193	35	15	243
	% within INCOME	79.4%	14.4%	6.2%	100.0%
	% of Total	29.7%	5.4%	2.3%	37.4%
1501 to 3000	Count	80	122	10	212
	% within INCOME	37.7%	57.5%	4.7%	100.0%
	% of Total	12.3%	18.8%	1.5%	32.6
3001 and above	Count	68	67	60	195
	% within INCOME	34.9%	34.4%	30.8%	100.0%
	% of Total	10.5%	10.3%	9.2%	30.0%
TOTAL	Count	341	224	85	650
	% within INCOME	52.5%	34.5%	13.1%	100.0%
	% of Total	52.5%	34.5%	13.1%	100.0%

5.1.6b. The Chi-square Values of the Responses

Item	*Value*
Calculated Value	181.957
Standard table value	13.28
Degrees of freedom	4
Levels of Significance	0.01

5.1.7. The Occupational Background Vs Opinions of the Respondents with Respect to the Monitoring of Balawadees

In order to study the influence of occupational background on the opinions of the respondents with respect to the monitoring of balawadees, six items were constructed and provided to the respondents. The responses of the parents/ community members are analyzed and presented below :

As evident from above table majority of daily wage workers / labour and traditional professional with business category felt that monitoring in Balawadees Low. Only majority of the service respondents in (Govt, and Pvt) felt that monitoring in Balawadees is Medium.

The null hypothesis has been tested by chi-square non-parametric statistical technique and the results obtained are interpreted at 99% level of confidence.

5.1.7b. The Chi-square Values of the Responses

Item	*Value*
Calculated Value	109.843
Standard table value	16.81
Degrees of freedom	6
Levels of Significance	0.01

5.1.7a. Frequency Distribution and Percentages

OCCUPATION		MONITORING			Total
		Low	Medium	High	
Daily wage workers/labourers	Count	110	36	9	155
	% within OCCUPATION	71.0%	23.2%	5.8%	100.0%
	% of Total	16.9%	5.5%	1.4%	23.8%
Traditional Professionals	Count	122	75	15	212
	% within OCCUPATION	57.5%	35.4%	7.1%	100.0%
	% of Total	18.8%	11.5%	2.3%	32.6%
Service Govt./Pvt.	Count	65	69	61	195
	% within OCCUPATION	33.3%	35.4%	31.3%	100.0%
	% of Total	10.0%	10.6%	9.4%	30.05
Business	Count	44	44		88
	% within OCCUPATION	50.0%	50.0%		100.0%
	% of Total	6.8%	6.8%		13.5%
TOTAL	Count	341	224	85	650
	% within OCCUPATION	52.5%	34.5%	13.1%	100.0%
	% of Total	52.5%	34.5%	13.1%	100.0%

Since the calculated value is more than the table value, the null hypothesis is rejected indicating that "There is an association between the occupational background of the respondents and their opinions about the monitoring of balawadees".

5.2.1. Age Background Vs Opinions of the Respondents with Respect to the Quality of Infrastructure Facilities in Balawadees

In order to study the influence of age background on the opinions of the respondents with respect to the quality of infrastructure facilities in balawadees seven items were constructed and provided to the respondents. The responses of the parents / community members are analyzed and presented below :

5.2.1a. Frequency Distribution and Percentages

AGE in years		*QUA.INFR*			*Total*
		Low	*Medium*	*High*	
21-30	Count	51	49	30	130
	% within AGE	39.2%	37.7%	23.1%	100.0%
	% of Total	7.8%	7.5%	4.6%	20.0%
31-40	Count	56	84	37	177
	% within AGE	31.6%	47.5%	20.9%	100.0%
	% of Total	8.6%	12.9%	5.7%	27.2%
41-50	Count	69	95	49	213
	% within AGE	32.4%	44.6%	23.0%	100.0%
	% of Total	10.6%	14.6%	7.5%	32.8%
51 and above	Count	52	47	31	130
	% within AGE	40.0%	36.2%	23.8%	100.0%
	% of Total	8.0%	7.2%	4.8%	20.0%
TOTAL	Count	228	275	147	650
	% within AGE	35.1%	42.3%	22.6%	100.0%
	% of Total	35.1%	42.3%	22.6%	100.0%

As seen in the above table majority of respondents from the age group of 21 to 30 years and from 51 years and above group have given the opinion that Quality of Infrastructural facilities in Balawadees is Low. The majority of respondents from the age group of 31to 40 years and 41 to 50 years age group opined that the quality of infrastructural facilities is medium.

5.2.1b. The Chi-square Values of the Responses

Item	*Value*
Calculated Value	6.107
Standard table value	12.59
Degrees of freedom	6
Levels of Significance	Not significant

The null hypothesis has been tested by chi-square non-parametric statistical technique and the results obtained are interpreted at 95% level of confidence.

Since the calculated value is less than the table value, the null hypothesis is accepted. Therefore, it can be inferred that "There is no association between the Age background of the respondents and their opinions about the quality of infrastructure facilities in balawadees".

5.2.2. Gender Background Vs Opinions of the Respondents with Respect to the Quality of Infrastructure Facilities in Balawadees

In order to study the influence of Gender background on the opinions of the respondents with respect to the quality of infrastructure facilities in balawadees seven items were constructed and provided to the respondents. The responses of the parents / community members are analyzed and presented below :

As seen from the above table majority of male and female respondents have felt that Quality of the Quality of Infrastructural facilities in Balawadees is Medium indicating need to improve it.

5.2.2a Frequency Distribution and Percentages

GENDER		QUA.INFR			*Total*
		Low	*Medium*	*High*	
Male	Count	113	146	66	325
	% within GENDER	34.8%	44.9%	20.3%	100.0%
	% of Total	17.4%	22.5%	10.2%	50.0%
Female	Count	115	129	81	325
	% within GENDER	35.4%	39.7%	24.9%	100.0%
	% of Total	17.7%	19.8%	12.5%	50.0%
TOTAL	Count	228	275	147	650
	% within GENDER	35.1%	42.3%	22.6%	100.0%
	% of Total	35.1%	42.3%	22.6%	100.0%

5.2.2b. The Chi-square Values of the Responses

Item	*Value*
Calculated Value	2.599
Standard table value	5.99
Degrees of freedom	2
Levels of Significance	0.05

The null hypothesis has been tested by chi-square non-parametric statistical technique and the results obtained are interpreted at 95% level of confidence.

Since the calculated value is less than the table value, the null hypothesis is accepted i.e., "There is no association between the gender background of the respondents and their opinions about the quality of infrastructure facilities in balawadees".

5.2.3. The Caste Background Vs Opinions of the Respondents with Respect to the Quality of Infrastructure Facilities in Balawadees

In order to study the influence of Caste background on the opinions of the respondents with respect to the quality of infrastructure facilities in balawadees seven items were constructed and provided to the respondents. The responses of the parents / community members are analyzed and presented below :

As seen from the above table majority of Scheduled castes, Scheduled Tribes and BC's felt that qualities is medium, while other caste respondents opined that the quality of infrastructure facilities is low.

Since the calculated value is less than the table value, the null hypothesis is accepted i.e., it is seen that "There is no association between the caste background of the respondents and their opinions about the quality of infrastructure facilities in balawadees".

5.2.3a. Frequency Distribution and Percentages

CASTE		QUA.INFR			*Total*
		Low	*Medium*	*High*	
SC	Count	75	97	49	221
	% within CASTE	33.9%	43.9%	22.2%	100.0%
	% of Total	11.5%	14.9%	7.5%	34.0%
ST	Count	59	82	33	174
	% within CASTE	33.9%	47.1%	19.0%	100.0%
	% of Total	9.1%	12.6%	5.1%	26.8%
BC	Count	64	73	54	191
	% within CASTE	33.5%	38.2%	28.3%	100.0%
	% of Total	9.8%	11.2%	8.3%	29.4%
Others	Count	30	23	11	64
	% within CASTE	46.9%	35.9%	17.2%	100.0%
	% of Total	4.6%	3.5%	1.7%	9.8%
TOTAL	Count	228	275	147	650
	% within CASTE	35.1%	42.3%	22.6%	100.0%
	% of Total	35.1%	42.3%	22.6%	100.0%

5.2.3b. The Chi-square Values of the Responses

Item	*Value*
Calculated Value	9.858
Standard table value	12.59
Degrees of freedom	6
Levels of Significance	0.05

5.2.4. Religious Background Vs Opinions of the Respondents with Respect to the Quality of Infrastructure Facilities in Balawadees

In order to study the influence of Religious background on the opinions of the respondents with respect to the quality of infrastructure facilities in balawadees seven items were constructed and provided to the respondents. The responses of the parents / community members are analyzed and presented below :

As seen from the above table majority from Muslims felt that Quality of Infrastructural facilities in Balawadees is Low. Majority of Hindus and Christians felt that Quality of Infrastructural facilities in Balawadees is Medium.

5.2.4b. The Chi-square Values of the Responses

Item	*Value*
Calculated Value	26.693
Standard table value	16.81
Degrees of freedom	6
Levels of Significance	0.01

Since the calculated value is more than the table value, the null hypothesis is rejected and it is concluded that "There is an association between the religious background of the respondents

5.2.4a. Frequency Distribution and Percentages

RELIGION		*QUA.INFR*			*Total*
		Low	*Medium*	*High*	
Muslims	Count	51	49	30	130
	% within RELIGION	39.2%	37.7%	23.1%	100.0%
	% of Total	7.8%	7.5%	4.6%	20.0%
Hindus	Count	56	84	37	177
	% within RELIGION	31.6%	47.5%	20.9%	100.0%
	% of Total	8.6%	12.9%	5.7%	27.2%
Christians	Count	69	95	49	213
	% within RELIGION	32.4%	44.6%	23.0%	100.0%
	% of Total	10.6%	14.6%	7.5%	32.8%
Others	Count	52	47	31	130
	% within RELIGION	40.0%	36.2%	23.8%	100.0%
	% of Total	8.0%	7.2%	4.8%	20.0%
TOTAL	Count	228	275	147	650
	% within RELIGION	35.1%	42.3%	22.6%	100.0%
	% of Total	35.1%	42.3%	22.6%	100.0%

and their opinions about the quality of infrastructure facilities in balawadees".

5.2.5. Education Background Vs Opinions of the Respondents with Respect to the Quality of Infrastructure Facilities in Balawadees

In order to study the influence of Education background on the opinions of the respondents with respect to the quality of infrastructure facilities in balawadees seven items were constructed and provided to the respondents. The responses of the parents / community members are analyzed and presented below :

5.2.5a. Frequency Distribution and Percentages

EDUCATION		*QUA.INFR*			*Total*
		Low	*Medium*	*High*	
Non Literates	Count	116	125	73	314
	% within EDUCATION	36.9%	39.8%	23.2%	100.0%
	% of Total	17.8%	19.2%	11.2%	48.3%
5 years of Schooling	Count	78	127	54	259
	% within EDUATION	30.1%	49.0%	20.8%	100.0%
	% of Total	12.0%	19.5%	8.3%	39.8%
6 to 10 years of Schooling	Count	29	16	18	63
	% within EDUCATION	46.0%	25.4%	28.6%	100.0%
	% of Total	4.5%	2.5%	2.8%	9.7%
11 to 15 years of Schooling	Count	5	7	2	14
	% within EDUCATION	35.7%	50.0%	14.3%	100.0%
	% of Total	8%	1.1%	3%	2.2%
TOTAL	Count	228	275	147	650
	% within EDUCATION	35.1%	42.3%	22.6%	100.0%
	% of Total	35.1%	42.3%	22.6%	100.0%

As seen from above table majority non-literates 5 years schooling respondents said that Quality of Infrastructural facilities in Balawadees is Medium.

Majority from of 6 to 10 years schooling respondent felt that quality is low. 50% of respondent with 11 to 15 years of schooling said that quality of Infrastructural facilities in Balawadees is Medium.

5.2.5b. The Chi-square Values of the Responses

Item	*Value*
Calculated Value	13.804
Standard table value	12.59
Degrees of freedom	6
Levels of Significance	0.05

The null hypothesis has been tested by chi-square non-parametric statistical technique and the results obtained are interpreted at 95% level of confidence.

As the calculated value is more than the table value, the null hypothesis is rejected and it is concluded that "There is an association between the Educational background of the respondents and their opinions about the quality of infrastructure facilities in balawadees".

5.2.6. The Income Background Vs Opinions of the Respondents with Respect to the Quality of Infrastructure Facilities in Balawadees

In order to study the influence of Income background on the opinions of the respondents with respect to the quality of infrastructure facilities in balawadees seven items were constructed and provided to the respondents. The responses of the parents / community members are analyzed and presented below :

As seen from the above table majority of respondent with low income upto Rs.1500 said that the Quality of Infrastructural facilities in Balawadees is Low. Majority from the monthly income between Rs 1501 to 3000 and 3001 and above group felt that the Quality of Infrastructural facilities in Balawadees is Medium.

Since the calculated value is less than the table value, the null hypothesis is accepted and it is concluded that "There is no association between the Income background of the respondents and their opinions about the quality of infrastructure facilities in balawadees".

5.2.6a. Frequency Distribution and Percentages

INCOME in Rupees per month		*QUA.INFR*			*Total*
		Low	*Medium*	*High*	
Upto 1500	Count	98	96	49	243
	% within INCOME	40.3%	39.5%	20.2%	100.00%
	% of Total	15.1%	14.8%	7.5%	37.4%
1501 to 3000	Count	64	105	43	212
	% within INCOME	30.2%	49.5%	20.3%	100.0%
	% of Total	9.8%	16.2%	6.6%	32.6%
3001 and above	Count	66	74	55	195
	% within INCOME	33.8%	37.9%	28.2%	100.0%
	% of Total	10.2%	11.4%	8.5%	30.0%
TOTAL	Count	228	275	147	650
	% within INCOME	35.1%	42.3%	22.6%	100.0%
	% of Total	35.1%	42.3%	22.6%	100.0%

5.2.6b. The Chi-square Values of the Responses

Item	*Value*
Calculated Value	11.228
Standard table value	13.28
Degrees of freedom	4
Levels of Significance	0.05

5.2.7. The Occupation Background Vs Opinions of the respondents With Respect to the Quality of Infrastructure Facilities in Balawadees

In order to study the influence of Occupation background on the opinions of the respondents with respect to the quality of infrastructure facilities in balawadees seven items were constructed and provided to the respondents. The responses of the parents / community members are analyzed and presented below :

As evident from above table majority of all the different categories of occupational groups supported the view that quality of infrastructure facilities is medium.

5.2.7b. The Chi-square Values of the Responses

Item	*Value*
Calculated Value	4.109
Standard table value	12.59
Degrees of freedom	6
Levels of Significance	Not significant

Since the calculated value is less than the table value, the null hypothesis is accepted and it is concluded seen that "There is no association between the occupation background of the respondents and their opinions about the quality of infrastructure facilities in balawadees".

5.2.7a. Frequency Distribution and Percentages

OCCUPATION		*QUA.INFR*			*Total*
		Low	*Medium*	*High*	
Daily wage Workers/Labourers	Count	59	64	32	155
	% within OCCUPATION	38.1%	41.3%	20.6%	100.0%
	% of Total	9.1%	9.8%	4.9%	23.8%
Traditional Professionals	Count	71	97	44	212
	% within OCCUPATION	33.5%	45.8%	20.8%	100.0%
	% of Total	10.9%	14.9%	6.8%	32.6%
Service Govt./Pvt.	Count	64	79	52	195
	% within OCCUPATION	32.8%	40.5%	26.7%	100.0%
	% of Total	9.8%	12.2%	8.0%	30.0%
Business	Count	34	35	19	88
	% within OCCUPATION	38.6%	39.8%	21.6%	100.0%
	% of Total	5.2%	5.4%	2.9%	13.5%
TOTAL	Count	228	275	147	650
	% within OCCUPATION	35.1%	42.3%	22.6%	100.0%
	% of Total	35.1%	42.3%	22.6%	100.0%

5.3.1. Age Background Vs Opinions of the Respondents with respect to Teacher Participation in Balawadees

In order to study the influence of the age background on the opinions of the respondents with respect to the Teacher participation in balawadees, seven items were constructed and provided to the respondents. The responses of the parents/ community members are analyzed and presented below :

5.3.1a. Frequency Distribution and Percentages

AGE in years		*TEAC.PAR*			*Total*
		Low	*Medium*	*High*	
21-30	Count	60	54	16	130
	% within AGE	46.2%	41.5%	12.3%	100.0%
	% of Total	9.2%	8.3%	2.5%	20.0%
31-40	Count	62	100	15	177
	% within AGE	35.0%	56.5%	8.5%	100.0%
	% of Total	9.5%	15.4%	2.3%	27.2%
41-50	Count	70	88	55	213
	% within AGE	32.9%	41.3%	25.8%	100.0%
	% of Total	10.8%	13.5%	8.5%	32.8%
51 and above	Count	99	20	11	130
	% within AGE	76.2%	15.4%	8.5%	100.0%
	% of Total	15.2%	3.1%	17%	20.0%
TOTAL	Count	291	262	97	650
	% within AGE	44.8%	40.3%	14.9%	100.05
	% of Total	44.8%	40.3%	14.9%	100.0%

As seen from the above table majority of respondents from the age group of 21 to 30 years and 51 years and above felt that Teacher participation is low. While majority from age group 31 to 40 and 41 to 50 said that Teacher participation is medium.

Since the calculated value is more than the table value, the null hypothesis is rejected, and it is concluded that there is an association between the Age background of the respondents and their opinions about the Teacher participation in balawadees".

5.3.1b. The Chi-square Values of the Responses

Item	*Value*
Calculated Value	96.917
Standard table value	16.81
Degrees of freedom	6
Levels of Significance	0.01

5.3.2. The Gender Background Vs Opinions of the Respondents with respect to the Teacher Participation in Balawadees

In order to study the influence of the Gender background on the opinions of the respondents with respect to the Teacher participation in balawadees, seven items were constructed and provided to the respondents. The responses of the parents/ community members are analyzed and presented below :

5.3.2a. Frequency Distribution and Percentages

GENDER		*TEAC.PAR*			*Total*
		Low	*Medium*	*High*	
Male	Count	206	87	32	325
	% within GENDER	63.4%	26.8%	9.8%	100.0%
	% of Total	31.7%	13.4%	4.9%	50.0%
Female	Count	85	175	65	325
	% within GENDER	26.2%	53.8%	20.0%	100.0%
	% of Total	13.1%	26.9%	10.0%	50.0%
TOTAL	Count	291	262	97	650
	% within GENDER	44.8%	40.3%	14.9%	100.05
	% of Total	44.8%	40.3%	14.9%	100.0%

As evident from the above table majority of Male respondents felt that Teacher participation is low. Majority of Female respondents felt that Teacher participation of in Balawadees is Medium, indicating the need to improve Teacher Participation.

5.3.2b. The Chi-square Values of the Responses

Item	*Value*
Calculated Value	91.097
Standard table value	9.21
Degrees of freedom	2
Levels of Significance	0.01

As the calculated value is more than the table value, the null hypothesis is rejected and is concluded that, "There is an association between the Gender background of the respondents and their opinions about the Teacher participation in balawadees".

5.3.3. The Caste Background and Opinions of Parents and Community Members with respect to the Teacher Participation in Balawadees

In order to study the influence of caste background and the opinion of the respondents with respect to the Teacher participation in balawadees, seven items were constructed and provided to the respondents. The responses of the parents/community members are analyzed and presented below :

As shown in the above table majority of SC's BC and OC said that Teacher participation in Balawadees is low. Only the majority of STs said that teacher participation is medium.

As the calculated value is more than the table value, the null hypothesis is rejected and is concluded that "There is an association between the caste background of the respondents and their opinions about the Teacher participation in balawadees".

5.3.3a. Frequency Distribution and Percentages

CASTE		*TEAC.PAR*			*Total*
		Low	*Medium*	*High*	
SC	Count	112	83	26	221
	% within CASTE	50.7%	37.6%	11.8%	100.0%
	% of Total	17.2%	12.8%	4.0%	34.0%
ST	Count	28	137	9	174
	% within CASTE	16.1%	78.7%	5.2%	100.0%
	% of Total	4.3%	21.1%	1.4%	26.8%
BC	Count	103	30	58	191
	% within CASTE	53.9%	15.7%	30.4%	100.0%
	% of Total	15.8%	4.6%	8.9%	29.4%
OC	Count	48	12	4	64
	% within CASTE	75.0%	18.8%	6.3%	100.0%
	% of Total	7.4%	1.8%	6%	9.8%
TOTAL	Count	291	262	97	650
	% within CASTE	44.8%	40.3%	14.9%	100.05
	% of Total	44.8%	40.3%	14.9%	100.0%

5.3.3b. The Chi-square Values of the Responses

Item	*Value*
Calculated Value	196.862
Standard table value	16.81
Degrees of freedom	6
Levels of Significance	0.01

5.3.4. The Religious Background Opinions of Parents and Community Members with respect to Teacher Participation in Balawadees

In order to study the influence of the Religious background and the opinion of the respondents with respect to the Teacher participation in balawadees, seven items were constructed and provided to the respondents. The responses of the parents/ community members are analyzed and presented below :

As seen from the above table majority of Muslims respondents along with Christians felt the Teacher participation is low. Majority of Hindus said that felt the Teacher participation in Balawadees in Medium.

44.4% of respondents from other religion felt that teacher participation is low.

5.3.4b. The Chi-square Values of the Responses

Item	*Value*
Calculated Value	89.985
Standard table value	16.81
Degrees of freedom	6
Levels of Significance	0.01

5.3.4a. Frequency Distribution and Percentages

RELIGION		*TEAC.PAR*			*Total*
		Low	*Medium*	*High*	
Muslims	Count	120	114	26	260
	% within RELIGION	45.2%	43.8%	10.0%	100.0%
	% of Total	18.5%	17.5%	4.0%	40.0%
Hindus	Count	114	123	23	260
	% within RELIGION	43.8%	47.3%	8.8%	100.0%
	% of Total	17.5%	18.9%	3.5%	40.0%
Christians	Count	49	16	47	112
	% within RELIGION	43.8%	14.3%	42.0%	100.0%
	% of Total	7.5%	2.5%	7.2%	17.2%
Others	Count	8	9	1	18
	% within RELIGION	44.4%	50.0%	5.6%	100.0%
	% of Total	1.2%	1.4%	2%	2.8%
TOTAL	Count	291	262	97	650
	% within RELIGION	44.8%	40.3%	14.9%	100.05
	% of Total	44.8%	40.3%	14.9%	100.0%

As the calculated value is more than the table value, the null hypothesis is rejected, and is concluded that "There is an association between the Religious background of the respondents and their opinions about the Teacher participation in balawadees.

5.3.5. The Educational Background Vs Opinions of the Respondents with respect to the Teacher Participation in Balawadees

In order to study the influence of the Educational background on the opinions of the respondents with respect to the Teacher participation in balawadees, seven items were constructed and provided to the respondents. The responses of the parents/ community members are analyzed and presented below :

5.3.5a. Frequency Distribution and Percentages

EDUCATION		*TEAC.PAR*			*Total*
		Low	*Medium*	*High*	
Non Literate	Count	194	86	34	314
	% within EDUCATION	61.8%	27.4%	10.8%	100.0%
	% of Total	29.8%	13.2%	5.2%	48.3%
5 years of Schooling	Count	76	164	19	259
	% within EDUCATION	29.3%	63.3%	7.3%	100.0%
	% of Total	11.7%	25.2%	2.9%	39.8%
6 to 10 years of Schooling	Count	7	12	44	63
	% within EDUCATION	11.1%	19.0%	69.8%	100.0%
	% of Total	1.1%	1.8%	6.8%	9.7%
11 to 15 years of Schooling	Count	14			14
	% within EDUCATION	100.0%			100.0%
	% of Total	2.2%			2.2%
TOTAL	Count	291	262	97	650
	% within EDUCATION	44.8%	40.3%	14.9%	100.05
	% of Total	44.8%	40.3%	14.9%	100.0%

As seen from the above table majority of literate category of 11 to 15 years schooling group felt the Teacher participation is Low. The majority from 5 years of schooling category felt that

Teacher participation is Medium. The majority from 6 to 10 years of schooling category felt that Teacher participation is High. Indicating strong influence of Education on opinions.

5.3.5b. The Chi-square Values of the Responses

Item	*Value*
Calculated Value	262.223
Standard table value	16.81
Degrees of freedom	6
Levels of Significance	0.01

Because the calculated value is more than the table value, the null hypothesis is rejected, indicating that "There is an association between the Educational background of the respondents and their opinions about the Teacher participation in balawadees".

5.3.6. The Income Background Vs Opinions of the Respondents with respect to Teacher Participation in Balawadees

In order to study the influence of the income background on the opinions of the respondents with respect to the Teacher participation in balawadees, seven items were constructed and provided to the respondents. The responses of the parents/ community members are analyzed and presented below :

As seen from the above table majority of respondents from the monthly wage of Rs 1500 and second group of Rs.1501 to 3000 felt that teacher participation in Balawadees is Medium. Majority of respondent from income group of Rs 3000 and above monthly income said that Teacher participation in Balawadees is low.

As the calculated value is more than the table value, the null hypothesis is rejected, and it is concluded that "There is an

5.3.6a. Frequency Distribution and Percentages

INCOME in Rupees per month		*TEAC.PAR*			*Total*
		Low	*Medium*	*High*	
Upto 1500	Count	104	114	25	243
	% within INCOME	42.8%	46.9%	10.3%	100.0%
	% of Total	16.0%	17.5%	3.8%	37.4%
1501 to 3000	Count	81	118	13	212
	% within INCOME	38.2%	55.7%	6.1%	100.0%
	% of Total	12.5%	18.2%	2.0%	32.6%
3001 and above	Count	106	30	59	195
	% within INCOME	54.4%	15.4%	30.3%	100.0%
	% of Total	16.3%	4.6%	9.1%	30.0%
TOTAL	Count	291	262	97	650
	% within INCOME	44.8%	40.3%	14.9%	100.05
	% of Total	44.8%	40.3%	14.9%	100.0%

association between the income background of the respondents and their opinions about the Teacher participation in balawadees".

5.3.6b. The Chi-square Values of the Responses

Item	*Value*
Calculated Value	96.532
Standard table value	13.28
Degrees of freedom	4
Levels of Significance	0.01

5.3.7. The Occupational Background Vs Opinions of the Respondents with respect to Teacher Participation in Balawadees

In order to study the influence of the occupational background on the opinions of the respondents with respect to the Teacher participation in balawadees, seven items were constructed and provided to the respondents. The responses of the parents/ community members are analyzed and presented below :

As seen from the above table majority of Daily Wage Workers / labourers and Traditional Professional Group felt that it is Medium. The majority of Service respondents and Business Category felt that Teacher participation is Low.

5.3.7b. The Chi-square Values of the Responses

Item	*Value*
Calculated Value	271.935
Standard table value	16.81
Degrees of freedom	6
Levels of Significance	0.01

5.3.7a. Frequency Distribution and Percentages

OCCUPATION		*TEAC.PAR*			*Total*
		Low	*Medium*	*High*	
Daily wage Workers/Labourers	Count	64	67	24	155
	% within OCCUPATION	41.3%	43.2%	15.5%	100.0%
	% of Total	9.8%	10.3%	3.7%	23.8%
Traditional Professionals	Count	33	161	18	212
	% within OCCUPATION	15.6%	75.9%	8.5%	100.0%
	% of Total	5.1%	24.8%	2.8%	32.6%
Service Govt./Pvt.	Count	107	33	55	195
	% within OCCUPATION	54.9%	16.9%	28.2%	100.0%
	% of Total	16.5%	5.1%	8.5%	30.0%
Business	Count	87	1		88
	% within OCCUPATION	98.9%	1.1%		100.0%
	% of Total	13.4%	2%		13.5%
TOTAL	Count	291	262	97	650
	% within OCCUPATION	44.8%	40.3%	14.9%	100.05
	% of Total	44.8%	40.3%	14.9%	100.0%

As the calculated value is more than the table value, the null hypothesis is rejected, and is concluded that "There is an association between the occupational background of the respondents and their opinions about the Teacher participation in balawadees".

5.4.1. The Age background vs Opinion of the Respondents with respect to the Learning Environment in Balawadees

In order to study the influence of the Age background on the opinions of the respondents with respect to the Learning Environment in balawadees, five items were constructed and provided to the respondents. The responses of the parents and community members are analyzed and presented below :

5.4.1a. Frequency Distribution and Percentages

AGE in years		*LEAR.ENV*			*Total*
		Low	*Medium*	*High*	
21 to 30	Count	74	34	22	130
	% within AGE	56.9%	26.2%	16.9%	100.0%
	% of Total	11.4%	5.2%	3.4%	20.0%
31 to 40	Count	74	87	16	177
	% within AGE	41.8%	49.2%	9.0%	100.0%
	% of Total	11.4%	13.4%	2.5%	27.2%
41 to 50	Count	83	53	77	213
	% within AGE	39.0%	24.9%	36.2%	100.0%
	% of Total	12.8%	8.2%	11.8%	32.8%
51 and above	Count	81	29	20	130
	% within AGE	62.3%	22.3%	15.4%	100.0%
	% of Total	12.5%	4.5%	3.1%	20.0%
TOTAL	Count	312	203	135	650
	% within AGE	48.0%	31.2%	20.8%	100.0%
	% of Total	48.0%	31.2%	20.8%	100.0%

As seen in the above table majority of respondents from the age group of 21 to 30 years and 31 to 40 years and 51 years and above have given the opinion that the Learning Environment in

Balawadees is Low. Only of respondent from age group 31 to 40 said that Learning Environment in Balawadees is medium.

5.4.1b. The Chi-square Values of the Responses

Item	*Value*
Calculated Value	76.802
Standard table value	16.81
Degrees of freedom	6
Levels of Significance	0.01

Because the calculated value is more than the table value, the null hypothesis is rejected, and is concluded that "There is an association between the age background of the respondents and their opinions about the Learning environment in balawadees".

5.4.2. The Gender, Background Vs the Opinions of the Respondents with respect to the Learning Environment in Balwaldies

The responses of the respondents are analysed and presented below :

5.4.2a. Frequency Distribution and Percentages

GENDER		*LEAR.ENV*			*Total*
		Low	*Medium*	*High*	
Male	Count	195	84	46	325
	% within GENDER	60.0%	25.8%	14.2%	100.0%
	% of Total	30.0%	12.9%	7.1%	50.0%
Female	Count	117	119	89	325
	% within GENDER	36.0%	36.6%	27.4%	100.0%
	% of Total	18.0%	18.3%	13.7%	50.0%
TOTAL	Count	312	203	135	650
	% within GENDER	48.0%	31.2%	20.8%	100.0%
	% of Total	48.0%	31.2%	20.8%	100.0%

As seen in the above table majority of the male respondent felt that Learning Environment in Balawadees is Low. Majority of female respondent felt that Learning Environment in Balawadees is Medium.

5.4.2b. The Chi-square Values of the Responses

Item	*Value*
Calculated Value	39.231
Standard table value	9.21
Degrees of freedom	2
Levels of Significance	0.01

As the calculated value is more than the table value, the null hypothesis is rejected, indicating that "There is an association between the Gender background of the respondents and their opinions about the learning environment in balawadees centers.

5.4.3. The Caste Background Vs the Opinions of the Respondents with respect to the Learning Environment in Balwaldies

The responses of the respondents are analysed and presented below :

As seen from the above table majority of Scheduled Caste's, STs and other caste groups felt the Learning Environment in Balawadees is Low. Majority of Schedule Tribes felt that the Learning Environment in Balawadees is low. Majority of Backward class felt that learning Environment in Balawadees is High.

Because the calculated value is more than the table value, the null hypothesis is rejected and is conclude that "There is an association between the caste background of the respondents and their opinions about the learning environment in balawadees".

5.4.3a. Frequency Distribution and Percentages

CASTE		LEAR.ENV			Total
		Low	Medium	High	
SC	Count	112	70	39	221
	% within CASTE	50.7%	31.7%	17.6%	100.0%
	% of Total	17.2%	10.8%	6.0%	34.0%
ST	Count	86	75	13	174
	% within CASTE	49.4%	43.1%	7.5%	100.0%
	% of Total	13.2%	11.5%	2.0%	26.8%
BC	Count	66	48	77	191
	% within CASTE	34.6%	25.1%	40.3%	100.0%
	% of Total	10.2%	7.4%	11.8%	29.4%
Others	Count	48	10	6	64
	% within CASTE	75.0%	15.6%	9.4%	100.0%
	% of Total	7.4%	1.5%	9%	9.8%
TOTAL	Count	312	203	135	650
	% within CASTE	48.0%	31.2%	20.8%	100.0%
	% of Total	48.0%	31.2%	20.8%	100.0%

5.4.3b. The Chi-square Values of the Responses

Item	*Value*
Calculated Value	87.434
Standard table value	16.81
Degrees of freedom	6
Levels of Significance	0.01

5.4.4. The Religious Background Vs the Opinions of the Respondents with respect to the Learning Environment in Balwaldies

The responses of the respondents are analysed and presented below :

As seen form the above table majority Muslims and other caste category felt that Learning Environment in Balawadees Low. While majority of Hindus said that felt that Learning Environment in Balawadees is Medium. Majority of Christian has said felt that Learning Environment in Balawadees is high.

5.4.4b. The Chi-square Values of the Responses

Item	*Value*
Calculated Value	150.333
Standard table value	16.81
Degrees of freedom	6
Levels of Significance	0.01

The null hypothesis has been tested by chi-square non-parametric statistical technique and the results obtained are interpreted at 99% level of confidence.

Since the calculated value is more than the table value, the null hypothesis is rejected, and is concluded that "There an

5.4.4a. Frequency Distribution and Percentages

RELIGION		*LEAR.ENV*			*Total*
		Low	*Medium*	*High*	
Muslims	Count	157	63	40	260
	% within RELIGION	60.4%	24.2%	15.4%	100.0%
	% of Total	24.2%	9.7%	6.2%	40.0%
Hindus	Count	107	122	31	260
	% within RELIGION	41.2%	46.9%	11.9%	100.0%
	% of Total	16.5%	18.8%	4.8%	40.0%
Christians	Count	31	18	63	112
	% within RELIGION	27.7%	16.1%	56.3%	100.0%
	% of Total	4.8%	2.8%	9.7%	17.2%
Others	Count	17		1	18
	% within RELIGION	94.4%		5.6%	100.0%
	% of Total	2.6%		2%	2.8%
TOTAL	Count	312	203	135	650
	% within RELIGION	48.0%	31.2%	20.8%	100.0%
	% of Total	48.0%	31.2%	20.8%	100.0%

association between the Religious background of the respondents and their opinions about the learning environment in balawadee centers".

5.4.5. The Educational Background Vs Opinions of the Respondents with respect to the Learning Environment in Balwaldies

The responses of the respondents are analysed and presented below :

5.4.5a. Frequency Distribution and Percentages

EDUCATION		*LEAR.ENV*			*Total*
		Low	*Medium*	*High*	
Non Literates	Count	193	78	43	314
	% within EDUCATION	61.5%	24.8%	13.7%	100.0%
	% of Total	29.7%	12.0%	6.6%	48.3%
5 years of Schooling	Count	117	111	31	259
	% within EDUCAITON	45.2%	42.9%	12.0%	100.0%
	% of Total	18.0%	17.1%	4.8%	39.8%
6-10 years of Schooling	Count	.	8	55	63
	% within EDUCATION		12.7%	87.3%	100.0%
	% of Total		1.2%	8.5%	9.7%
11-15 years of Schooling	Count	2	6	6	14
	% within EDUATION	14.3%	42.9%	42.9%	100.0%
	% of Total	3%	9%	9%	2.2%
TOTAL	Count	312	203	135	650
	% within EDUCATION	48.0%	31.2%	20.8%	100.0%
	% of Total	48.0%	31.2%	20.8%	100.0%

As seen from above table majority of majority of non-literate group and five years schooling group felt that Learning Environment in Balawadees is Low. The majority respondent with 6 to 10 years schooling and 11 to 15 years schooling said that Learning Environment in Balawadees is High.

Because the calculated value is more than the table value, the null hypothesis is rejected, and is conclude that "There is an association between the Educational background of the respondents and their opinions about the learning environment in balawadees centers".

5.4.5b. The Chi-square Values of the Responses

Item	*Value*
Calculated Value	223.482
Standard table value	16.81
Degrees of freedom	6
Levels of Significance	0.01

5.4.6. The Income Background Vs Opinions of the Respondents with respect to the Learning Environment in Balwaldies

The responses of the respondents are analysed and presented below :

As seen from the above majority of respondents with monthly income upto Rs 1500 said that the Learning Environment in Balawadees is Low. Majority from the monthly income between 1501 to 3000 felt that Learning Environment in Balaweadees is Medium. Majority of respondent with monthly income of Rs. 3001 and above felt that Learning Environment is High.

5.4.6b. The Chi-square Values of the Responses

Item	*Value*
Calculated Value	101.379
Standard table value	13.28
Degrees of freedom	4
Levels of Significance	0.01

5.4.6a. Frequency Distribution and Percentages

INCOME in Rupees Per month		*LEAR.ENV*			*Total*
		Low	*Medium*	*High*	
Upto 1500	Count	155	51	37	243
	% within INCOME	63.8%	21.0%	15.2%	100.0%
	% of Total	23.8%	7.8%	5.7%	37.4%
1501 to 3000	Count	91	101	20	212
	% within INCOME	42.9%	47.6%	9.4%	100.0%
	% of Total	14.0%	15.5%	3.1%	32.6%
3001 and above	Count	66	51	78	195
	% within INCOME	33.8%	26.2%	40.0%	100.0%
	% of Total	10.2%	7.8%	12.0%	30.0%
TOTAL	Count	312	203	135	650
	% within INCOME	48.0%	31.2%	20.8%	100.0%
	% of Total	48.0%	31.2%	20.8%	100.0%

As the calculated value is more than the table value, the null hypothesis is rejected and is conclude that "There is an association between the income background of the respondents and their opinions about the learning environment in balawadees.

5.4.7. The Occupational Background Vs Opinions of the Respondents with respect to the Learning Environment in Balwaldies

The responses of the respondents are analysed and presented below :

5.4.7a. Frequency Distribution and Percentages

OCCUPATION		*LEAR.ENV*			*Total*
		Low	*Medium*	*High*	
Daily wages Workers/Laboures	Count	90	40	25	155
	% within OCCUPATION	58.1%	25.8%	16.1%	100.0%
	% of Total	13.8%	6.2%	3.8%	23.8%
Traditional Professionals	Count	96	95	21	212
	% within OCCUPATION	45.3%	44.8%	9.9%	100.0%
	% of Total	14.8%	14.6%	3.2%	32.6%
Service Govt./Pvt.	Count	67	47	81	195
	% within OCCUPATION	34.4%	24.1%	41.5%	100.0%
	% of Total	10.3%	7.2%	12.5%	30.0%
Business	Count	59	21	8	88
	% within OCCUPATION	67.0%	23.9%	9.1%	100.0%
	% of Total	9.1%	3.2%	1.2%	13.5%
TOTAL	Count	312	203	135	650
	% within OCCUPATION	48.0%	31.2%	20.8%	100.0%
	% of Total	48.0%	31.2%	20.8%	100.0%

As seen from above table majority of respondents from daily wage workers / labourers traditional professionals and Business respondents felt that Learning Environment is Low. Only majority of service respondents (Govt, Pvt) felt that Learning Environment is high.

Majority of the respondents from all occupation opined that the Learning Environment in Balawadees is low.

5.4.7b. The Chi-square Values of the Responses

Item	*Value*
Calculated Value	96.420
Standard table value	16.81
Degrees of freedom	6
Levels of Significance	0.01

Because the calculated value is more than the table value, the null hypothesis is rejected and is concluded that "There an association between the occupational background of the respondents and their opinions about the learning environment in balawadees centers".

THE STATUS OF BALAWADIES – AN OVERVIEW

The Origin

The Balawadee pre-primary school for urban slum children has started in the year 1967. This project of educating the urban slum early childhood children started in 11 cities in India at once, our twin cities was one of those 11 cities in India. In the beginning it was limited to coverage of old city locality; due to good response in neighbouring areas in the twin cities the public demand for Balawadees increased in other areas or localities. This lead to extension of Balwadees. The government created additional post of project officer, Dy. Project Officer and field level staff. The programmes of Balawadees were more useful to children of slums in twin cities. In the year 1981 total Balawadees under UCD were

350. The Balwadees were managed by local welfare socities or Mahila Mandalies of the concerned areas.

Urban Community Development

The urban community project was established in the Municipal Corporation of Hyderabad for implementing Urban Poverty Alleviation programmes for the people below poverty line living in the slums of the twin cities of Hyderabad and Secunderabad. The UCD in Hyderabad was started in the year 1967 with the aim of creating a sense of social coherence on neighbourhood basis, developing a sense of belonging to the urban community in every family, bringing about a change in attitudes, developing local initiatives and ensuring fuller utilization of the technical and welfare services through self help. Towards this end, the project has been developing various methodologies, normally employed in social planning such as corporate civic action, promoting national integration, concentrating on people initiative, organization, self help and mutual aid. Since the project is an integral part of Municipal Corporation its emphasis is on creating civic consciousness and motivating people to improve their conditions of lives.

Activities of the UCD

The UCD in twin cities had been focusing on a variety of activities, since its inception. Broadly, the activities are :

(a) Environmental sanitation
(b) Family welfare activities
(c) Supplementary feeding programmes
(d) Recreational and cultural activities
(e) Education activities
(f) Economic activities
(g) Construction of community halls

Under Educational programmes Balawadees is one of the very important component. This educational programme for pre primary level is intended to mould the child at the pre-school age. Educational programmes like Balawadees, cruches, Anganwadies, coaching centers, adult literacy centers, reading rooms and libraries, community TV sets under matching grants film shows, etc. in slums are taken up based on the local needs and the peoples involvement. The Balawadees and Anganwadies cover the children of the age group 3 to 6 years, while the creshes are for the children below 3 years. Health care, nutrition, physical development, literacy development, development of sports and cultural talents, inculcation of good habits and discipline etc., are taken care of at these centers, which are run in collaboration with the local voluntary organizations. The Anganwadies have been working under the ICDS programme and urban community development project co-ordinates with local voluntary organizations.

Teachers

The welfare societies and Mahila Mandals in different localities appoint the teachers in Balawadees. The teacher is essentially from the local community. These teachers were called initially as voluntary workers. Their appointments were approved by UCD. In the year 1967 the honorarium was Rs.175/- per month and was increased to 250 in 1985. Subsequently the total honorarium was increased to Rs.500 per month out of which Rs.350 was paid by the UCD and Rs.150 was paid by Local Community to the teacher. During the year 1995-96 the MCH absorbed many of these teachers in the permanent posts of MCH: as per their qualifications and Govt. guidelines. The classes under Balawadee scheme are normally conducted in the community halls constructed by UCD.

5.6 Teachers reactions on the functioning of the Balawadees :

The investigator interviewed all the teachers of 20 Balawadee centers with the help of open ended interview schedule.

According to this study twenty centers were established during the period between 1985 to 1993. It is quite likely that some of the centers in slums were closed and some others were freshly established. It is also likely that there have been changes in the continuation of teachers. Therefore, the information given in the section is based on the interviews conducted during 1998-99.

In each center, there are about 25 to 35 students and the class is are conducted mostly in the community hall constructed by UCD. Under mid day meals programme the UCD supplied nutritious food to the extent of 200 grams per day per student consisting of wheat, corn, ground nuts and jaggery. The community halls have fairly good facilities of drinking water, electricity, ventilation, toilets etc. According to the teachers the curriculum followed corresponds to the kindergarten system of education. Medical facilities required by Balawadees are taken care by the Government hospitals located near by the existing slums. The teachers are of the opinion that there is no built-in mechanism for neither pre-service training nor in-service training of teachers.

The infrastractural facilities such as table and chair for the teacher black board, pieces of chalk to write and other essential requirements are met. The students generally selected on the floor. Most of the teachers have passed S.S.C. and a few are intermediate and degree holders. Normally UCD project team visit Balawadee centers once in a month, accompanied by community members of the concerned Balawadee. The teachers expressed dissatisfaction about the low payment of salaries. There is a regular interaction of the teacher with the parents of the children studying in Balawadees, because either they come to Balawadee to drop the child in school or to pick them up in the evening. This provides constant opportunity for the teachers to exchange ideas, needs and problem etc., about the children for their progress.

Participation of International Bodies

Women and children programmes assumed greater importance with the association of UNICEF in 1977. The Urban Planners particularly the social planners world over have been evincing keen interest in the programmes of Women and Children. The UNICEF also contributed financially. The overseas Development Authority (ODA) UK was also associated with the child and women welfare.

After the Closer of ODA project the Balwadees centers were handed over to Women and Child Welfare Department. Majority of this centers were converted in to Anganwadi centers depending upon Anganwadi project annually some Balawadees ware taken into the fold. According to the annual report of 2003 there are 27 Balawadees functioning in the twin cities of Hyderabad and Secunderabad.

During 1979 – 81 UNICEF contributed 50% of expenditure of UCD programmes and the remaining 50% was borne by the State Government. There after during 1983-96 overseas administration department of United kingdom gave liberal assistance to UCD amounting to Rs.1.5 crores.

Funding of Balawadees:

The Balawadees are community based centers. The members of the voluntary organizations like Mahila Mandalies, Welfare Societies etc., are in constant interaction with the Balawadees.

According to 1979-80 Annual Report of the UCD project 167 Balawadees were functioning at various places in twin cities with strength of 4000 children of 3 to 5 years age group where in free medical check up, free mid-day meals etc were provided to them.

No balawadee is inspected by UCD directly and only local community and the voluntary organization did the monitoring work.

Source: (Annual Report of UCD, MCH and Interviews with the project officers).

6

The Summary Conclusions and Discussion

6.1. Overview

The present study is basically a survey from married and unmarried men and women who are educated and employed in Hyderabad and Secunderabad belonging to different age, caste, religion education income and professional groups, about issues such as availability of infrastructural facilities, health care, curriculum suitability, monitoring, quality of infrastructural facilities, teacher participation and learning environment issues related to the Balawadee pre-primary educational institutions in Twin cities of Hyderabad and Secunderabad.

The National policy on education (1986) has given a great deal of importance to early childhood care and education (ECCE). It views ECCE as an important input in the strategy of human resources development, as a feeder and support programme for Primary Education and as a support service for working women of the disadvantaged section of society.

The quality of pre-primary education depends upon the quality of infrastructural facilities curriculum, contents, health care available, monitoring pattern existing, teacher participation in the programme and the learning environment prevailing in the schools.

Good quality pre-school experience improves enrolment in primary school and also increases the retention rate, to meet the target of universal elementary education. Hence, the relevance of the study.

Balawadee Centers caters to the educational need of 3 to 6 years old age group of children living in urban slums of twin cities of Hyderabad and Secunderabad. This study is important as there is need for developing the system of early childhood education particularly in urban slum areas since, almost all the women go to work and also the home and community situations are not congenial for the healthy growth of children. Further, the educational, health and nutritional services are not effectively reaching the slum children. Organized pre-school activity will help the children of disadvantaged sections in reaching the educational, health and other welfare services effectively.

6.2 Statement of the Problem :

"The working of Balawadees in twin cities of Hyderabad and Secunderabad : A critical study of the opinions of community members and parents."

6.3 Objectives of the Study :

The following are the objectives of the study :

(i) To find out and asses the opinions of community members and parents on the infrastructure facilities available in Balawadees under the UCDEP programme.

(ii) To find out and asses the opinions of community members and parents on the availability about the health care facilities of Balawadees under UCDEP.

(iii) To enquiry into and asses the opinions of community members and parents on the suitability of the curriculum of Balawadee centers under UCDEP.

(iv) To study asses the opinions of community members and parents on monitoring pattern followed in Balawadee centers under UCDEP.

(v) To study and asses the opinions of community members and parents on Quality of Infrastructural facilities available in Balawadees under UCDEP.

(vi) To understand and asses the opinions of community members and parents on Teacher participation existing under Balawadee System of UCDEP.

(vii) To find out and asses the opinions of community members and parents on Learning Environment existing in Balawadees under UCDEP.

6.4 Hypotheses :

Corresponding to the objectives stated, the following hypothesis are formulated :

(i) There is no association between the opinions of community members and parents on infrastructural facilities existing and the attributes of respondents like age, gender, caste, religion, education, income and occupation

(ii) There is no association between the opinions of community members and parents on Healthcare facilities in the Balawadees and the age, gender caste, religion, education, income and occupational facts about respondents.

(iii) There is no association between the opinions of community members and parents on Curriculum Contents followed and the different attributes of respondents like age, gender, caste, religion, education, income and occupational qualities.

(iv) There is no association between the opinions of community members and parents on monitoring pattern followed in the and the attributes of respondents like age, gender, caste, religion, education, income and occupational qualities.

(v) There is no association between the opinions of community members and parents on the quality of infrastructural facilities existing in different Balawadees and the age, gender, caste, religion, education, income and occupational qualities of the respondents.

(vi) There is no association between the opinions of community members and parents on teacher participation in the Balawadees schools and the attributes of respondents like age, gender caste, religion, education income and occupational qualities.

(vii) There is no association between the opinions of community members and parents on learning environment existing in Balawadee Pre-primary schools and the age, gender, caste, religion, education, income and occupational facts of the respondents.

6.5 Sample

In the twin cities of Hyderabad and Secunderabad there are Twenty Balawadee Centres. Fifteen are in Hyderabad and five are in Secunderabad. All the twenty centers have been studied. In selecting the sample from among the parents and community members, random sampling method was used. The sample include men and women of married and unmarried status with different monthly income and different occupations. It consists of two categories of people who are associated with working of Balawadees. They are parents of the children studying in Balawadees and the community members who are local residents staying in the neighbourhood of Balawadees rendering social service for the welfare of the people. The details of the respondents is given in chapter III. Out of thousand opinionnaires, five hundred were given to parents and five hundred to community members. Out of them hundred and sixty one respondents from Secunderabad and four hundred and eight nine respondents from Hyderabad were received. In total six hundred and fifty responses were taken for the study from both the cities.

6.6 Tools

After the review of literature and having consulted the experts and the officials of UCDEP, a baseline survey was conducted with the help of a questionnaire (Appendix III). This questionnaire contained four parts I, II, III, IV. With the help of this questionnaire discussions were held with teachers of Balawadees, fifty parents and fifty community members in the viscinity of twenty Balawadee centers under study. Based on the insights gained and knowledge of the status of Balawadees a detailed opioinnaire was prepared (Appendix I).

This opinionnaire (Appendix I) served as the main tool of the investigation.

This study is a descriptive research, it finds out the existing position of twenty Balawadees located in Hyderabad and Secunderabad, popularly known as twin cities. This study will probe into the opioinions / perceptions of the community members and parents.

The opinionnaire is comprehensive and covered the following aspects :

(A) Personal Data : Personal information of the respondents which include age, sex, caste, educational level, employment, marital status, number of children, etc.

(B) Opinionnaire on the following subjects is collected:

(i) Availability of infrastrucutral facilities
(ii) Availability of health care
(iii) Suitability of curriculum
(iv) Monitoring on Balawadees centers
(v) Quality of infrastructural facilities
(vi) Teacher participation under Balawadees
(vii) Learning environment existing in Balawadees pre-primary schools.

6.7 Statistical Techniques Used

Coded data was entered on separate code-sheet and analyzed using the computer facility. Data were analyzed by means of frequency tabulation.

Item analysis, counting the percentages of each responses to the opinion was carried independently from the respondents of twin cities of Secunderabad and Hyderabad and also the cumulative analysis of the responses of the respondents put together.

To measure the association between independent and dependent variables the study applied cumulative analysis and x^2 (chi-square) test to estimate the opinions of respondents from varied backgrounds on aspects under investigation.

6.8 Testing of Hypotheses

Conclusions are drawn against various hypotheses. Detailed analysis was made in chapter IV & V. Based on the levels of significance the conclusions are drawn.

The conclusions are generally drawn at 1% level of significance. If any conclusion is drawn at 5% level, specific reference is made against that conclusion.

6.8.1 *Hypothesis-1*

"There is no association between the opinion of community members and patents on the infrastructural facilities existing and the attributes of respondents like age, gender, caste, religion, education, income and occupation".

This hypothesis is related to availability of infrastructural facilities in the Balawadees centers of Hyderabad and Secunderabad. The items studied under this were adequacy of size and ventilation of class rooms, availability of drinking water and toilet facilities, availability of lighting and electricity, adequacy of fencing / protection facilities, adequacy of seating arrangement to the children, adequacy of play material and play ground, adequacy of teaching Aids Black board and visual charts.

A null hypothesis is formulated to study this problem, revealed association between the two sets of variables. Details given in Chapter - IV.

Conclusions

(i) The infrastructural facilities existing varies with the age group of respondents. The young and middle aged group felt that infrastractural facilities were of middle level, but the older people strongly felt it as low.

(ii) Over whelming number of respondents irrespective of Gender felt, the infrastractural facilities are of medium level and not satisfactory.

(iii) Caste has influenced the opinions of the respondents. The SC and ST respondents said the availability of infrastructure is of medium level. While OC's clearly said it is low. The BC's did not agree with this and felt it is of high level.

(iv) Religion has influenced the opinions of respondents as three major religions completely differed with one another, indicating variation in the existing infrastructural facilities in the Balawadees.

(v) The educational level of respondents influenced their opinions on the question of availability of infrastructural facilities. Majority of all non-literates and well educated together felt that the facilities are low.

(vi) The two low income groups influenced on the desirability of rising the infrastructural facilities while high income group did not agree with this.

(vii) All the occupational groups belonging to, the daily wage and low income and traditional professionals along with business group of respondents indicated the need to improve the facilities to high level. The government service respondents did not agree on this.

6.8.2 Hypothesis - 2

"There is no association between the opinions of community members and parents on the health care facilities in the Balawadees and the age, gender, caste, religion, education, income and occupational facts about respondents".

This hypothesis is related to availability of health care facilities to the people of Balawadee vicinity areas. The items studied under this hypothesis were. The adequacy of awareness training given to parents and community members about health care food and nutrition, adequacy of care taken about bathing and dressing of children, adequacy of guidance given to the respondents about preventive and curative allments like polio, triple antigen etc., adequacy of measures taken for curative diseases of children with respect to fever, cold caugh and skin diseases, frequency of visits to balawadees vicinity areas to maintain health care, meticulous maintenance of health status program, adequacy of supply of nutritious food to children, availability of first-aid facilities, level of participation of non governmental organizations like lions clubs, rotary club etc. to maintain health care of children, regularity of health check up for children, availability of medicines to children at the time of need.

The above questions were studied on the respondents, the details are given in chapter-V. The respondents were classified on the basis of age, gender, caste, religion, education, income and occupations.

A null hypothesis is formulated to study this issue, revealed association between the two sets of variables.

Conclusions

(a) Age has influenced options on desirability of improving the health care facilities. Most of the age groups belonging to very young and very old age group of respondents felt that health care is not satisfactory.

(b) The involvement of Men against women is more as they felt that health care is low while women felt it to be of medium or average level.

(c) Most of the caste groups preferred for rising the health care to high level.

(d) Respondents belonging to the Muslims and Hindus along with other caste respondents wanted health care to be improved to high level. The Christians did not agree with this view.

(e) Irrespective of educational back ground of respondents most of them felt the need to rise the Health Care facilities to highlevel. Only one group of respondents belong to 6 to 10 years schooling did not agree with above said three groups.

(f) The three different income groups gave different opinions contradicting one another on Health Care indicating the influence of income of respondents.

(g) Most of the professional groups were not satisfied with health care facilities in Balawadees. But the government service respondents did not agree with those three groups.

6.8.3 Hypothesis - 3

"There is no association between the opinions of community members and parents on Curriculum Contents followed and the different attributes of respondents like age, gender, caste, religion, education, income and occupational qualities".

The above hypothesis is related to the curriculum followed in the Balawadees centers. The dimensions of curriculum studied were, the time table of the balawadees centers were helpful to the parents or not, adequacy of test books used, the availability of teacher guides, manuals and resource books, the adequacy of need based nature of curriculum, on question of nature of classroom activity, adequacy of classroom climate, emphasis givens to three R^s, suitability of curriculum. The detailed analysis of each of these problems is dealt at Chapter – IV.

A null hypothesis is formulated to study this issue revealed association between the two sets of variables.

Conclusions

(a) Most of the age groups were strongly critical about curriculum suitability existing. They rated it as low; indicating the need to review curriculum followed in Balawadies.

(b) Female respondents felt that curriculum suitability is low while male counter parts felt it as medium, indicating the influence of gender.

(c) Irrespective of caste all group felt desirability of improving curriculum suitability from low level to high level (Significant at 5% level).

(d) The two major religious groups felt curriculum suitability as low while the third religious group differed indicating influence of religion.

(e) Irrespective of literacy level of respondents all educational groups said that curriculum suitability is not satisfactory or of medium level.

(f) The different income groups together influenced opinions in favour of improving the curriculum suitability from low level to high level.

(g) Irrespective of occupational status of respondents all supported the need for rising the curriculum suitability to high level from existing low standard.

6.8.4 Hypothesis - 4

"There is no association between the opinions of community members and parents on monitoring pattern followed in the Balawadees and the attributes of respondents like age, gender, caste, religion, education, income and occupational qualities".

This hypothesis is related to monitoring on the administrative and academic functioning of Balawadees in twin cities. The items studied under this were : regularity of academic evaluation, proper utilization of funds by Balawadees, participation of Community members in the monitoring of Balawadees, the teachers need for more support and guidance, the need for convergence of government bodies with NGO's for improving its functioning, and on weather once a month parent teacher meet is conducted.

A null hypothesis is formulated to study this problem it revealed association between the two sets of variables.

Conclusions

(a) Irrespective of age most of them influenced the opinions favouring improvement of regularity of evaluation from low to high.

(b) Both male and female respondents supported the view of rising the existing low level of monitoring to high level.

(c) Irrespective of caste all respondents said that monitoring is low indicating no influence of caste on opinions.

(d) Opinion varies with religion of respondents as Muslims and Hindus both strongly favoured high monitoring in place of low standard existing. But Christian did agree for this.

(e) Irrespective educational status of respondents most of them felt that monitoring is low.

(f) Most of the respondents belonging to different income groups felt that monitoring on Balawadees is low.

(g) Majority of different occupational groups felt that monitoring is low; while only one group of government service respondents differed, in strengthening the need to improve quality and quantity in monitoring.

6.8.4 Hypothesis - 5

"There is no association between the opinions of community members and parents on the quality of infrastructural facilities existing in different Balawadees and the age, gender, caste, religion, education, income and occupational qualities of the respondents".

The quality of infrastructure studied in detail in Chapter – IV were : quality of classrooms their size and ventilation, quality of drinking water and toilet facilities, quality of electricity connection, quality of fencing around premises, quality of teaching arrangements, quality of play material and size of play ground, and quality of teaching aids, back board, visual charts.

A null hypothesis formulated to study this issue confirmed no association between two sets of variables in four cases out of seven.

Conclusions

(a) Most of the respondents belonging to different age structure strongly favoured improvement of the quality from present low level to high level. How ever other two groups also supported this view. No group disagreed with opinion of rising the quality from low to high level (Significant at 5% level). There is no association between the age of respondents and their opinions.

(b) Irrespective of gender both male and female respondents influenced opinions to improve quality infrastructural to high level from average level existing (Significant at 5% level). Indicating no association between gender and opinions.

(c) Most of the respondents belonging to different castes supported need to improve quality to high level (Significant at 5% level). From existing medium level. indicating no association between the caste and the opinions.

(d) Half of the major religious groups felt that quality is not satisfactory or low. The other half felt that it is of medium level indicating association between religion and opinions of respondents.

(e) Education of respondents did not influence opinions as all the different educational categories felt the need to improve quality to high level (Significant at 5% level) from existing medium level.

(f) The respondents with low income reported to be strongly in favour of improvement of quality from low to high level, however other two income groups supported this view. The Chi-square test indicated association between the income and opinions of respondents.

(g) All different four occupational groups strongly agreed that the quality of infrastructure is not satisfactory and needs to be up graded. The Chi-square revealed no association between the occupational back ground of the respondents and there opinions on quality of infrastractural facilities.

6.8.5 Hypothesis - 6

"There is no association between the opinions of community members and parents on the teacher participation in the Balawadee schools and the attributes of respondents like age, gender caste, religion, education, income and occupational qualities".

The different dimensions studied under this is in detail at Chapter–V were : Methods of teaching, the relationship between the teacher and children the use of play way materials by teacher, using disciplinary and punishment mechanisms, the rate of involvement of teacher and need for in serve training of teachers.

A null hypothesis is formulated related to Teacher Participation in Balawadee preprimary schools; On testing the null hypothesis the association between two variables is confirmed.

Conclusions

(a) There is influence of age on opinions of respondents as the very young and aged respondents together felt that Teacher Participation is low while other two groups felt it as medium.

(b) More number of male respondents said that Teacher Participation is low while females said it is medium, this indicates the influence of gender, on opinion.

(c) There is no influence of caste on opinions on Teacher Participation. Majority of all castes felt that Teacher Participation is low.

(d) Out of four major religious groups three groups felt that Teacher Participation is low, influencing opinions towards rising Teacher Participation.

(e) Educational level of respondents has no impact on their opinions, irrespective of educational difference most of the respondents supported for rising Teacher Participation to high level.

(f) The different income level respondents strongly felt to enhance level of Teacher Participation to high standard, indicating influence of income on opinions.

(g) The government service and business occupational groups strongly preferred that Teacher Participation must improve from low to high level, while other groups also however supported this view.

6.8.7 Hypothesis - 7

"There is no association between the opinions of community members and parents on learning environment existing in

Balawadee Pre-primary schools and the age, gender, caste, religion, education, income and occupational facts of the respondents".

Hypothesis 7 is related to Learning Environment existing in Balawadees Pre-primary schools, the different problems studied in detail at Chapter – V were as follows, the behaviours of teacher towards children whether the children are not afraid of teacher, If teacher encourages children to attend to school, on the question weather the salary paid to teacher is reasonable, on question of need for rising the minimum qualification of teacher.

A null hypothesis is formulated to study the learning environment in Balawadee pre-primary schools, on testing it the association between two sets of variables is positively confirmed.

Conclusions

(a) Most of the very young and the aged respondents together felt that it is low. But only one out of 4 groups belonging to 31 to 40 years age group felt it differently.

(b) Male respondents were strong in favouring rise of Learning Environment from low to high level over female respondents.

(c) Most of the different caste respondents felt that Learning Environment is very low while only B.C's felt differently.

(d) On question of Learning Environment three major religious groups felt the need to improve it from prevailing low to high level. But Christians felt the opposite way.

(e) Educational level of respondent influenced opinions as respondents with minimum literacy said that Learning Environment is low while people with more educational qualifications felt that Learning Environment is high.

(f) The low income groups criticized Learning Environment existing as low while high income group felt it is high.

(g) Most of the three occupational groups influenced opinion upon rising Learning Environment from low to high while only one group of government service respondents felt opposite.

6.9 Major Conclusions

(I) On the question of availability of infrastructural facilities:

(i) The chi-squire test revealed an association between the age, gender, religion, education, income and occupation on the one side and availability of infrastructural facilities on the other.

(ii) The different age gender, education and income group of respondents felt that it is not satisfactory.

(iii) The different religions completely differed with one another indicating influence of religion on opinions.

  (a) Muslims felt it's status as very low

  (b) Hindu's felt it as medium

  (c) Christians felt it as of high standard

(iv) The different caste groups completely disagreed with each other indicating it's influences on opinions.

(v) There is significant association between different occupational groups and their opinions in favour of improving them to high level.

(II) On the question of availability of heath care facilities

(i) The chi-squire test revealed an association between the age, gender, religion, education, income and occupation on the one side and availability of health care facilities on the other.

(ii) All different age groups of respondents preferred to rise it from low level to high except the group belonging to 41 years to 50 years.

(iii) Men against women strongly felt that health care is low standard.

(iv) The caste has influenced their opinions as most of different caste respondents felt that it is low, but BC's felt the opposite way.

(v) All the three major religions differed in their opinion on health care indicating strong influence of religion on opinions.

(vi) Majority of all the different educational groups respondents felt that it needs to be improved form existing average level to high.

(vii) Income influenced opinions. Most of the different income groups felt the need to rise the health care facilities from low level to high.

(viii) Most professional groups strongly felt that health care is low satisfactory, but the Government / Private service respondents felt it as high requiring no effort to improve.

(III) Regarding curriculum suitability existing in Balawadee pre-primary Schools

(i) The chi-squire test revealed an association between the age, gender, religion, education, income and occupation on the one side and availability of curriculum suitability on the other.

(ii) The Chi-square test revealed there is an association between age, gender, religion, education, income and occupation on the one side and curriculum suitability on the other.

(iii) Gender did not have influence on opinions as both male and female respondents strongly felt it as low.

(iv) Irrespective of caste all respondents felt that curriculum suitability is low (Significant at 5% level).

(v) Most of major religions strongly felt that curriculum needs to be improved to high standard from existing low.

(vi) Irrespective of educational level of respondent all group said that curriculum suitability is not satisfactory.

(vii) All different income groups influenced opinions in favour of improving it form existing low standard to high standard.

(viii) Irrespective of occupational status all groups supported need for rising it from existing low to high standard. However business group felt it is unsatisfactory.

(IV) On question of monitoring standard existing on Balawadee Pre-primary schools :

(i) The chi-square test revealed that there is an association between the two variables on question of monitoring. The age, gender, religion, education, caste, income and occupations are associated with opinions on monitoring.

Most of all age groups of respondents influenced opinions favouring improvement in quality of monitoring from existing low to high level. No group disagreed with this.

(ii) Irrespective of gender both male and female respondents strongly felt that monitoring is of low level implicating need for training of the supervisory personnel entrusted with tasks of monitoring.

(iii) All the four caste groups strongly agreed that monitoring is of low level, indicating no influence of caste on opinions.

(iv) All religious groups except Christians strongly felt that monitoring is low.

(v) Most of the literacy groups felt that monitoring is low.

(vi) Most of all income groups strongly felt that monitoring is low level.

(vii) Most of occupational group of respondents clearly indicated that it is of low level.

(V) Regarding the question of quality of infrastructural facilities existing in Balawadees

(i) The chi-square test revealed that there is no association between age, gender, caste and occupation and the quality of facilities (Significant at 5% level).

Most of the age groups of respondents felt that quality of infrastructure is low.

(ii) Irrespective of gender all respondents felt that monitoring is of medium quality and not high quality (significant 5% level) indicating need for efforts to improve it.

(iii) Caste did not influence opinions as all caste respondents expressed the need to up grade quality of infrastructure from average level to high.

(iv) All the respondent belonging to different religions strongly agreed for the need to improve quality of facilities no religion disagreed for this statement.

(v) The respondent belonging to different educational levels agreed that quality of facilities are not satisfactory (Significant at 5% level). Indicating need for efforts to improve it.

(vi) The low income groups felt that quality of infrastructure as low. The other income groups agreed on this indicating no influence of income on opinions.

(vii) All the four occupational groups felt that quality is not satisfactory and that it needs to be upgraded (There is no assiociation between the occupation of the respondents and the quality of the infrastructure facilities).

(VI) On question of adequacy of teacher participation in the Balawadees programme

(i) The chi-square test revealed that there is an association between age, caste, religion, education, income and occupation and the teacher participation and the opinions of the respondents.

(ii) There is influence of age on responses as all age groups agreed that there is need for improving the adequacy of teacher participation in Balawadees to high level.

(iii) There is influence of gender on opinions as men were more strong in saying it is low. The females however supported it.

(iv) There is no influence of caste on opinions as all caste groups felt that teacher participation is of low.

(v) Irrespective of religion all respondent supported for revision of teacher participation to improve its adequacy.

(vi) Irrespective of educational level of respondents all felt that teacher participation is of low adequacy except one group of 6 to 10 years education who differed.

(vii) There is no influence of income on respondents as all income groups favoured improvement of adequacy of teacher participation from low level to high.

(viii) No occupational group felt that teacher participation is high in adequacy. All groups favoured rising the adequacy of teacher participation indicating influence of occupation on opinions.

(VII) On question of adequacy of learning environment

(i) The Chi-square test revealed that there is an association between age, gender, caste, religion, education, income, occupation and learning environment.

(ii) Majority of different age groups strongly stated that learning environment is low.

(iii) While male respondents were more clear in criticizing the adequacy of learning environment in Balawadees female members felt it as of medium level.

(iv) Majority of caste groups felt that the learning environment prevailing is of low grade, only BC group felt it as high.

(v) Most of the religious respondent felt that learning environment needs to be upgraded to high level.

(vi) Educational Level of respondents influenced in favour of improving adequacy of learning environment from low to high standard.

(vii) Income of respondents influenced opinions as different income respondents felt differently.

(viii) Majority of all occupational groups felt that adequacy of learning environment in Balawadees is low. Only one group out of four groups felt that it is high, emphasizing the need to upgrade adequacy of learning environment.

6.10 Discussion

In conclusion, it could be said that the variables like age, gender, caste, religion, education, income and occupation of respondents had association with the opinions on questions of availability of infrastructural facilities in Balawadees, health care prevailing, curriculum suitability practised, monitoring provided, teacher participation existing and learning environment existing in Balawadees.

Only on question of quality of infrastructure existing in Balwadees the chi-square test revealed that there is no association between the following variables at 0.05% level of significance.

(a) between age and quality of infrastructure facilities
(b) between gender and quality of infrastructure facilities
(c) between caste and quality of infrastructure facilities
(d) between occupation and quality of infrastructure facilities.

The cumulative majority of respondents have clearly and definitely influenced opinions on stating that the administrative and academic practices and facilities are of low standard or level and are not even middle/ average level. Hence, there is a dire need to take up on priority basis the task of upgrading the infrastructural facilities, quality and quantity wise, in Balawadees with health care, curriculum suitability, monitoring, teacher participation and learning environment.

Majority of parents of the Balawadee Children and the community members of the vicinity areas of Balawadee's felt that the academic and administrative atmosphere is not satisfactory or rather the satisfaction is low. It is generally believed that there is positive association between good infrastructural facilities and high academic achievement and high enrolment and retention rates. But the study revealed that physical infrastructure facilities are of medium level. Cumulative majority of respondents stated that facilities are existing, but are not satisfactory. Lot of concern is shown by parents and community members for early childhood education. Hence, the constitutional aim of universalization of education will be a reality if there is improvement in infrastructural facilities in all the centers.

The common experience shows that development stems from good health and nutrition. We need to be aware of health needs of children. But, the cumulative majority of respondents stated that there is need to improve health care awareness and facilities in the urban slums of twin cities.

Regarding curriculum contents it is expressed by majority that it is not child centered. This shows the awareness among the people today.

On the question of monitoring on Balawadees it is observed that it is not satisfactory. It could be due to lack of proper training to the community members and the project evaluation staff who are entrusted with monitoring on Balawadees.

On question of quality of infrastructure, most of respondents felt that there is no quality in academic and administrative matters in Balawadee centers. The chi-square test revealed that there is no association between age variation versus the quality of facilities. Same findings are found between gender versus quality of facilities, caste versus quality of facilities and occupation versus quality of facilities. The level of comprehension of parents and community members regarding the quality of infrastructure facilities at pre-primary level could be the probable cause for their opinions.

Regarding teacher participation, majority of respondents said it is not satisfactory. Practical out look of people could be the cause for their opinions. The low monthly salary given to the teacher and low infrastractural facilities could also be the reasons for their opinions.

Finally, as far as learning environment is concerned no satisfaction is expressed by most of the respondents. The general awareness about the need and importance of the pre-primary education among the parents and community members could be the cause for their opinions. Hence, there is need to review the learning environment to bring about significant rise in developmental status of children.

We need to be aware of multiple needs if the child's survival is for growth and development, as well as for protection and participation. We need to take care of parents and community members and the realities of their lives into account. The Balawadee programme based on the needs of individual and the values of the society in which it is being implemented should deal with questions such as; what is the content of the programme? who is the recipient? what is the methodology? on whom it is to be implemented? who is the person providing it? and above all, how is the monitoring or evaluation is done, qualitatively and quantitatively?

Hence, a wholistic approach using value based contribution of research in science and technology provides a meaningful life to the child with varying needs. As we move forward to the next millennium we will find more families transitioning into new models of child rearing, and we must be ready to meet the challenges of addressing their needs and assisting the parents and community members to support children.

The educational status of slum children is very discouraging, it needs to be looked into on priority basis. The quality of inputs is important to bring about significant rise in developmental status of children's. There is need for reform in the working of Balawadee pre-primary schools keeping in view the constitutional requirements. The infrastractural facilities, health care, curriculum suitability, monitoring on Balawadees, quality of infrastractural facilities, teacher participation and learning environment deserves attention for drawing maximum benefits from this programme as, no satisfaction is expressed by the cumulative majority of parents and community members with regard to the existing academic and administrative functioning of the Balawadee pre-primary education system in twin cities of Hyderabad and Secunderabad.

6.11 Educational Implications

The following educational implications are drawn keeping the conclusions of the study in view.

1. The constitutional objective of compulsory and the free primary education upto the age of 14 years will be a reality if academic and administrative system of balawadees is improved to a high level.

2. Cumulative Majority of respondents opinion about academic and administrative system prevailing in Balawadees is not satisfactory or rather the satisfaction is low. If there is positive

change in above two areas it would result in absorbing all slum dweller children into main stream and leads to improvement in building human resource potential.

3. It would be ideal if some more incentives are arranged to the children and the parents to attract social and economically backward sections towards pre primary education of balawadees.

4. All parents play key role in the education of children and their health conditions. The parental orientation programme is essential for attaining maximum results for the programme of balawadees.

5. Since research in education proved that early childhood education is crucial in making the child resourceful, the government should give wide publicity and provide adequate finance for effective functioning and maintenance of balawadees and similar such schools.

6. The pre-primary sections and baby creches must be attached to all primary schools by the government so that the older children can bring the younger children along with them to school. This arrangement will encourage girls education and will lead to eliminating gender discrimination from the society. Further, this promotes social integration.

6.12 Limitations of the Study

The present investigation has the following limitations. In view of the limited time and resources.

1. The study is confined to the Balawadee Centers of UCDEP in Twin cities of Hyderabad and Secunderabad.

2. The scope of the study is limited to the Balawadee Centre under UCDEP, and but not under the other agencies of management.

3. The investigation is confined to pre primary education programme undertaken under UCDEP of MCH in Andhra Pradesh.

6.13 Suggestions for Further Research

1. There is need to evaluate the perceptions of officials involved in monitoring of Balawadees under UCD Department of MCH to improve the quality of Balawadees.

2. There is need to study the role of voluntary organizations in extending support to early childhood care and education in urban slums of the twin cities to widen the support system.

3. There is need to study the Akshara Jyothi and other similar programmes existing in the urban slums of twin cities for the care and education of pre primary children.

4. There is need to study the job satisfaction of the teachers working under this scheme of Balawadees.

5. A comparative study of Balawadees and Anganwadies in respect of their strengths and weaknesses is needed.

Appendix

Oppinionnaire

Part - A

BIO-DATA OF THE PARENT/COMMUNITY MEMBER

1. Name :
2. Location of Center :
3. Age :
4. Sex :
5. Qualification :
6. Religion :
7. Social Status :
8. Occupation :
9. Income :
10. Counting and Assets :

PART – B

Opinions about infrastructure and physical facilities of Balwadi. Please Read the following and encircle your opinion

	Strongly Agree	*Agree*	*Undecided*	*Dis Agree*	*Strongly Disagree*
(A) Availability of infrastructure facilities					
1. The number of class rooms their size and ventilation are adequate and sufficient	SA	A	UD	D	SD
2. The drinking water & toilets facilities in the Balwadi serve the need of the children	SA	A	UD	D	SD
3. The lighting (Electricity connection available and ventilation are sufficient.	SA	A	UD	D	SD
4. The fencing around the premises and other protection facilities are sufficient	SA	A	UD	D	SD
5. The seating arrangement of children in the class room is up to the mark.	SA	A	UD	D	SD
6. The play-material and play ground in the balawadee are appropriate to the number of students.	SA	A	UD	D	SD
7. The teaching aids black board, visual charts are good in number	SA	A	UD	D	SD

(Contd.)

(Contd. Part- B)

(B) Quality of infrastructure facilities	*Strongly Agree*	*Agree*	*Undecided*	*Dis Agree*	*Strongly Disagree*
1. The quality of class rooms their size and ventilation are adequate and sufficient	SA	A	UD	D	SD
2. The quality of drinking water & toilets facilities in the Balawadee serve the need of the children	SA	A	UD	D	SD
3. The quality of Electricity connections available and ventilation are sufficient.	SA	A	UD	D	SD
4. The quality of fencing around the premises and other protection facilities are sufficient	SA	A	UD	D	SD
5. The quality of seating arrangement of children in the class room is up to the mark.	SA	A	UD	D	SD
6. The quality of play-material and play ground in the balawadee are appropriate to the number of students.	SA	A	UD	D	SD
7. The quality of teaching aids black board, visual charts are good in number	SA	A	UD	D	SD

(Contd.)

(Contd. Part- B)

	Strongly Agree	*Agree*	*Undecided*	*Dis Agree*	*Strongly Disagree*
(C) Health Care Facilities					
1. The awareness training given to parents/teachers about health care food nutrition are adequate.	SA	A	UD	D	SD
2. A special care is taken about bathing and dressing of children	SA	A	UD	D	SD
3. Sufficient guidance is given to parents/teachers about preventive and curative ailments like polio, triple antigen etc.	SA	A	UD	D	SD
4. The measures taken for curative diseases of children in Balwadi are appreciable with respect to fever, cold and cough skin diseases etc are taken care.	SA	A	UD	D	SD
5. Health care programmes/ visits are done frequently	SA	A	UD	D	SD
6. The health status program is maintained meticulously	SA	A	UD	D	SD
7. Nutritious food is supplied to the children	SA	A	UD	D	SD

(Contd.)

(Contd. Part- B)

	Strongly Agree	*Agree*	*Undecided*	*Dis Agree*	*Strongly Disagree*
8. First aid facilities are provided in the center.	SA	A	UD	D	SD
9. Frequent participation of NGO's like lions club/rotary	SA	A	UD	D	SD
10. Regular health check up is done to the children	SA	A	UD	D	SD
11. Medicines are supplied to children in time of need.	SA	A	UD	D	SD
(D) Curriculum Details					
1. The timing of the Balwadi are helping the parents enabling their children learn while the parents are busy.	SA	A	UD	D	SD
2. Text books are used.	SA	A	UD	D	SD
3. Teacher guides manuals and resource books are available in sufficient number.	SA	A	UD	D	SD
4. The content of curriculum is need based.	SA	A	UD	D	SD

(Contd.)

(Contd. Part- B)

	Strongly Agree	*Agree*	*Undecided*	*Dis Agree*	*Strongly Disagree*
5. Teaching activity in classroom is					
(i) Lecturing	SA	A	UD	D	SD
(ii) Group work	SA	A	UD	D	SD
(iii) Children mostly working on their own	SA	A	UD	D	SD
6. Classroom climate is	SA	A	UD	D	SD
(iv) Authoritative	SA	A	UD	D	SD
(v) Liberal/Democratic	SA	A	UD	D	SD
(vi) Highly Flexible	SA	A	UD	D	SD
7. More emphasis is given to three R's	SA	A	UD	D	SD
8. The curriculum adopted in these centers is suitable for the improvement of the children.	SA	A	UD	D	SD

(Contd.)

(Contd. Part- B)

	Strongly Agree	*Agree*	*Undecided*	*Dis Agree*	*Strongly Disagree*
(E) Monitoring					
1. Academic assessment and evaluation is being done regularly.	SA	A	UD	D	SD
2. Funds available under UCDEP are properly utilized	SA	A	UD	D	SD
3. The community members participation is up to the mark	SA	A	UD	D	SD
4. In the monitoring of Balwadi	SA	A	UD	D	SD
5. Teachers need more support and guidance for better teaching	SA	A	UD	D	SD
6. The convergence of Government bodies with NGO's will improve the working of Balwadi	SA	A	UD	D	SD
7. Once a month parent teacher meet is conducted	SA	A	UD	D	SD

(Contd.)

(Contd. Part- B)

	Strongly Agree	*Agree*	*Undecided*	*Dis Agree*	*Strongly Disagree*
(F) Teacher Performance/ Participation					
1. The method of teaching in these centers is appropriate	SA	A	UD	D	SD
2. The relation between the teacher and student is encouraging.	SA	A	UD	D	SD
3. The teaching learning environ-ment of the centers is positive	SA	A	UD	D	SD
4. The play-way materials are used by teachers regularly	SA	A	UD	D	SD
5. The disciplinary and punishment mechanisms are practiced by teacher.	SA	A	UD	D	SD
6. The rate of involvement of teacher is good.	SA	A	UD	D	SD
7. Teacher needs in-service training in					
(a) Methodology	SA	A	UD	D	SD
(b) Health care food and nutrition	SA	A	UD	D	SD

(Contd.)

(Contd. Part- B)

	Strongly Agree	*Agree*	*Undecided*	*Dis Agree*	*Strongly Disagree*
(G) Learning Environment					
1. The behavior of teacher towards children is positive	SA	A	UD	D	SD
2. Children are not afraid of teacher	SA	A	UD	D	SD
3. Teacher is one of the main reasons					
(i) The child goes to school	SA	A	UD	D	SD
(ii) The child does not go to school	SA	A	UD	D	SD
	SA	A	UD	D	SD
4. The salary paid to teachers is reasonable for the service rendered	SA	A	UD	D	SD
5. The minimum qualification of the teacher should be graduation	SA	A	UD	D	SD

Bibliography

1. Agarwal, J.C. 1986. 'National Policy on Education 1986 and Main recommendations of National Commission on Teachers, Doab house, New Delhi.
2. Agarwal, J.C. 1992. History and Philosophy of Pre-Primary and nursery education DOA BA house Nai Sark, Delhi.
3. Abstracts from International Journals, O.U.
4. Austin, G.R. 1976. Early Childhood Education An International Perspective, Academic Press. New York.
5. Butch, M.B. 1991. Fourth Survey of Educational Research NCERT, New Delhi.
6. Butch, M.B. 1996. Fifth Survey of Research Education. NCERT, New Delhi.
7. Bagai, R. 1988. Adult-child interaction in three communities, impleadors for children growth cognitive in social development Ph.D., Home SC University of Delhi (Govt.)
8. Belsky J. and Steinberg L.D. 1978. The effects of Daycare; a critical review child development
9. Best John, W. 1986. Research in Education, 5th Edition, Prentice Hall of India (Pvt.) Ltd., New Delhi.
10. Bhai Rangit. 1968. "The Systems of Pre-school Education in India" Voluntary efforts in pre-school Education, New Delhi.
11. Bloom, B. 1964. Stability and change in Human characteristics New York Willey.
12. Brown Fenbrenner, U. Is early intervention effective ? A report on longitudinal evaluation of pre-school programme,

office of child development, Department of Health, Education and Welfare, Washington D.C., 1974.

13. Bruce, D.Gross Man, Carol Keyes; Early Childhood Administration; Allyn and Bacon, INC. Boston London Sydney.
14. Centre for Educational Research and Innovation (CERI) 1981. Children and Society: Issues for Preschool Reforms. Organization for Economic Co-operation and Development, Paris.
15. Danny Barbara. 1983. Early Childhood Education organizing learning activities Mcmillan Publishing Co. Inc., New York.
16. Encyclopeadia of Education: Pargamon Series.
17. Gita Ramaswamy. The child and the law, A.P.Judicial Academy, Secunderabad 1996.
18. Glimpses of Hyderabad Urban Community Development by T.Rajagopala Chary, Director, Urban Community Development Projects MCH, 1983.
19. Government of India National Policy on Education 1986 programme of action 1992 New Delhi Ministry of Human Resources, Dept. of Education 1992, Indian Council of Child Welfare 1978 National Seminar on Education of the Teacher for the Pre-School Child. New Delhi.
20. Jagan Mohan, G. 2001. Early Childhood Education a Quality Study. The Journal of SCERT, A.P., Hyderabad.
21. Lazar, I. 1979. Lasting Effects after Pre-school: Summary Report. Department of Health. Education and Welfare, Pub.No.(OHDS) 79-30179, Washington DC. ERIC Document No.ED 175 523.
22. Lazerson, M. 1972. The Historical antecedents of early childhood education. In: Gordon I (ed.) 1972 Early Childhood Education. Seventy-first Yearbook of the National Society for the Study of Education. Part 2, University of Chicago, Illinois.
23. Manual, A. 1998. "Guidelines at a glance for the pre-school teacher" SRC AMS, Hyderabad.
24. Muralidharan, R. 1968. Personal Social Development of Indian Children Developmental norms of Indian Children.

25. Muralidharan, R. 1991. "Effect of pre-school Education on the language and intellectual development of under privileged children" NCERT (1984) in Buch, M.B. (Edu.) Fourth Survey of Research in Education, NCERT, New Delhi.
26. Muthayya, D.C. 1974. Naidu K.K. and Ranga Charyulu. Evaluation Programme of Child Welfare NIRD
27. Nagalaxmi, J. Establishing the Essentials for pre-primary education 1991. Ph.D. dissertation, O.U., Hyderabad.
28. National Institute of Educational planning and administration Education for all by 2000 AD – Indian Perspective New Delhi 1990 this book deals with different aspects of Educational Importance of Children.
29. Pakjam, G. 1978. Pre-basic education. In: Indian Counsil of Child Welfare 1978.
30. Petors, D.L. 1974. Daycare: the problem: The process the prospects childcare quarterly.
31. Pre-school Playgroups Association (in press) Playgroups in the Eighties.
32. Seminar report of Early childhood Education held in Andhra Pradesh in 1989.
33. Seminar report of Early childhood eduction held in Chennai 1999.
34. Skinner B.F. The technology of Teaching Newyork Appleton Century Crofts 1968
35. Shukla, P.D. The new education in India New Delhi Sterling Publishers Pvt. Ltd. 1988 consist relevant information on Indian situation.
36. Singh, K.K., Gopal, A.K. and Murthy, N.R. 1978. "Balwadees in India" an Evaluation Study NIPCD, New Delhi.
37. Somerset G 1976. Parents involvement in Early Childhood Education. Wellington Playcentre Association, Wellington, ERIC Document No.ED 156 317.
38. Sood, N. 1987. "Appraisal of pre-school education" in ICDS.
39. Spodek, Bernard. Early childhood education (Chapter 3) Eagle Wood Cliff, N.J., Prentice Hall, 1973.
40. Spodike, B. and H.J.Walberg. 1977. Early Childhood Education Issues and Insights Berkely, Salif, Mecutcham

41. Spodek, B.L. 1982. Education "Hand book of Research in Early Childhood Education". New York Free Press.
42. Tarapore, F.Z. "Study of Non-formal Pre-school components of ICDS.
43. The National Policy on education 1986.
44. Urban Community Development Brief Note MCH, 1996.
45. Moore, S. 1978 the persistence of preschool effort: A national collaborative study. Young children 33, 37: 65-71
46. Wood head M. 1979 pre-school Education in West Europe: Issues policies and Trends: A report of the council of Europe's project on pre-school Education, Long Men, London.
47. Ministry of HRD, 1986. The National Policy on education, India: Dept. of Education Govt. of India.
48. Ministry of Humal. Resource Development, 1986. National Policy on Education, India: Department of Education, Government *of* India.
49. Ministry of Human Resource Development, 1992. National Policy on Education: Programme of Action. India: Department of Education. Government of India.
50. Mishra, D. 1990. A study of the problems of pre-school education in the city of Cuttaek. M.Phil., Edu. Ravenshaw College, Cuttack.
51. Mishra, S. 1991. Effects of cognitive inter\'\:ntion training on intelligence and curiosity of pre-school children. M.Phil., Psy. Utkal Univ.
52. Mistry, Veena; Kaul, Sunjta and Dhar, Hansa, 1989. Indepth study of non-formal pre-school education component in Baroda Urban ICDS block. Independnet study. The Maharaja Sayajirao Univ. of Baroda.
53. Mohite, Prerana, 1990. Review of researches in early childhood care and education: A trend support. Independent study. The Maharaja Sayajirao Univ. Baroda.
54. Moore, S. 1978. The persistence of preschool effort: A national collaborative *s'udy.* Young children 33, 37: 65-71
55. Muralidharan, R. 1968. Personal Social Development of Indian Children Developmental norms of Indian Children.
56. Muralidharan, R. 1991. "Effect of pre-school Education on the language and intellectual development of under

privileged children" NCER T (1984) in Buch, M.B. (Edu.) Fourth Survey of Research in Education, NCERT, New Delhi.

57. Mura1idharan, Rajalakshmi and Misra, S. 1989. Home-based programme in child development. Independent study. New Delhi: National Council of Educational Research and Training.

58. Muralidharan, Rajalakshmi and Pankajam, G. 1988. An evaluation study of the different models of pre-school tcacher training programme from the point of view of their impact on children. Independent study. New Delhi: National Council of Educational Research and Training.

59. Murlidharan, Rajalakshmi and Upadhyay, G.C. 1992. "Effectiveness of toy-making compctitions in the States: An assessment". Independent study. N ~w Delhi: National Council of Educational Research and Training.

60. Murty, V. 1992. An investigation into the scholastic readiness of J:re-schooi children. Ph.D., Edu. Univ. *of* Bombay.

61. Muthayya, D.C. 1974. Naidu K.K. and Ranga Charyulu. Evaluation Programme of Child Welfare NIRD

62. Myers, R.G. 1988. Effects of early childhood intervention on primary school progress and performance in the developing countries. An updated paper presented at a seminar on the importance of nutrition and early stimulation for the education of chifdren in the Third World: Stockholm and High/Scope Educational Rcscarch Foundation, Ypsilanli, Mlchlgan (Mimeo).

63. Myers, R.G. 1992. The Twelve Who Survive: Strengthening programmes of early childhood development in the Third World. New York: Routledge in co-operation with UNESCO.

64. Myers, R.G. and Hertenberg, R. 1987. The Eleven Who Survive: Towards a re-examination of early childhood development programme option and costs. Washington, D.C.: Education and Training Series. World Bank Report No.: EDT 69.

65. Nagalaxmi, J. 1991. Establishing the Essentials for pre-primary education. Ph.D. *disseJ1ation,* O.U., Hyderabad. (d. Nat'ional Institute of Educational planning and administration

Education for all by 2000 AD - Indian P(.~rspcctivc New Dclhi 1990 this book dcals with different nspcl.:ts of' Edlll.:atiullalll11pOl'tan~c of'Childn:n.

66. Pakjam, G. 1978. P.e-basic education. In: Indian Council of Child Welfare 1978.
67. Pandey, H. 1989. Impact of the pre-school education component in integrated child development services programme on the cognitive development of children. Ph.D., I-lome Science, Avinashilingam'Institute for Home Science and Higher Education for Women.
68. Pankajam, G. et.a!., 1990. Child-care services in Tamilnadu. Indcpendent study, Madurai Kamaraj Univ.
69. Pattanaik, A. 1991. Effects of pre-school education on cognitive development of primary school children. Ph.D., Edu., Utkal Univ.
70. Petors, D.L. 1974. Daycare: the problem: The process the prospects childcare quarterly.
71. Rajagopala Chari. Ilydcrabad.1996. Urban Community Developmcnt Brief Notc MCH,
72. Rajagopala Chary, T. 1983. Glimpses of Hyderabad Urban Community Dcvelopli'tCn(Director, Urban Community Development Projccts f\.1CH.
73. Rajalakshmi, M. 1992. An assessment of the existing nursery education progrjlmme in Kerala. Ph.D., Edu., Univ. ofCalicut.
74. Ratnaik, Bijayalaxami, 1988. Cognitive and linguistic development processes in children's stories. Ph.d., Psy. Berhampur, Univ.
75. Rawal. U. 1992. An attempt in programmc cvaluation of a model remedial pre-school. M.Phil., Psy. Utkal Univ.
76. Regional Centre. 1991. ICDS: An appraisal in Bihar and Madhya Pradesh. Independent study. Lucknow: National Institute of Public Cooperation and Child Development.
77. Rights of the Child. 1991. World declaration and plan of action from the World Summit for Children. Convention on the rights of the child. Thl~ department of Women and Child Development, Government of India.

78. Seminar report of Early childhood education held in Cl1l'nnai Nov., 1999.
79. Seth, Kanta and Ahuja, Kavita, 1992. Minimum specifications for pre-schools, Independent study. New Delhi: national Council of Educational Research and Training.
80. Sdha. Poonam, 1991. Effect of pan:ntal interaction and educational intervcntion fur optimizing the integrated development of pre-school children. Ph.D., Edu. Panjab lJniv.
81. Sharma, Adarsh, 1990. Status of social componcnts of ICDS in Haryana rural projects Bhiwani and Adampur. Independent study. New Delhi: National Institute of Public Cooperation and Child Development
82. Sharma, Adarsh, 1992. National evaluation of integrated child development services. Independent study. New Delhi: National Institute of Public Cooperation and Child Development.
83. Sharma, Ranjana, 1992. Pre-school education: A comparative study of aided and unaided pre-schools in Pune City. M.Phi!., Edu., Indian Institute of Education, Pune.
84. Shukla, P.D. 1988. The new education in India New Delhi Sterling Publishers Pvt. Ltd. consist relevant information on Indian situation.
85. Singh, Anjali, 1987. Certain deprivation factors in language development in children.Ph.D., Psy. Univ. of Allahabad.
86. Singh, K.K., Gopal, A.K. and Murthy, N.R. Evaluation Study NIPCD, New Delhi. "Balwadees in India" an 1978.
87. Skinner B.F. 1968. The technology of Teaching New York Appleton Century Crofts.
88. Somerset, G. 1976. Parents involvement in Early Childhood Education. Wellington Playcentre Association, Wellington, ERIC Document No.ED 156317.
89. Sood, Neelam, 1987. An evaluation of non-formal pre-school education component in Mangolpuri ICDS block. Independent study. New Delhi: NatiQnal Institute of Public Cooperation and Child Development.
90. Sood, Neelam, 1992. Pre-school education in ICDS: An appraisal. Independent study. New Delhi: National Institute of Public Cooperation and Child Development.

91. Spodek, B.L. 1982. Education "Hand book of Research in Early Childhood Education". New York Free Press.
92. Spodek, Bernard. 1973. Early childhood education (Chapter 3) Eagle Wood Cliff, N.J., Prentice Hall.
93. Spod ike, B. and H.J .Walberg. 1977. Early Childhood Education Issues and Insights Berkel)', Salif, Mecutcham
94. Srilatha, G. 1988. Mother-child interaction during pre-school age in different socio-economic status groups. M.Phi!., Home Sc. Sri Yenkateswara Univ.
95. Srivastava, Sushila, 1992. A short-term longitudinal study of the impact of Tarapore, F.Z. "Study of Non-formal Pre-school components of ICDS.
96. Wood head M. 1979. Pre-school Education in West Europe: Issul s policies and Trends: A report of the council of Europe's project on pre-school Education, Long Men. London.

Index